Teamwork Plain an‹

What are the necessary ingredients which make a team of staff in schools successful? How can teamwork in schools be improved? In what ways does effective teamwork in schools result in more efficiency, more enjoyment, and more success? *Teamwork Plain and Simple* provides the answers to these questions, offering a fresh perspective on how teachers and school leaders can implement effective teamwork in schools.

Rooted in three decades of teaching and school leadership experience and drawing on his ground-breaking research through this essential text, **Dr Michael Harpham** identifies the five key ingredients that support effective teamwork in schools and offers over 40 situation-driven strategies to help you lead and develop your team. The chapters cover:

- Expectations of working and progressing as a team
- Team communication and interaction
- Team behaviours and building relationships
- Organisational infrastructure and team functionality
- Capacity and growing your team

Including a user-friendly audit to evaluate the efficacy of your team, as well as useful tips and practical case studies, this guide is a crucial read for any teacher or school leader who wishes to improve their organisation's teamwork.

Dr Michael Harpham is a headteacher, author, educational consultant, and Fellow of the Chartered College of Teaching. He is also Director of School Leader Development Ltd, a consultancy that specialises in training and coaching for school leaders and their teams. He is the author of *Progress Plain and Simple: What Every Teacher Needs to Know about Improving Pupil Progress* (2020) and *The School Leader's Year* (2021).

Teamwork Plain and Simple

5 Key Ingredients to Team Success in Schools

Michael Harpham

Routledge
Taylor & Francis Group

LONDON AND NEW YORK

Designed cover image: © Getty Images

First published 2023
by Routledge
4 Park Square, Milton Park, Abingdon, Oxon OX14 4RN

and by Routledge
605 Third Avenue, New York, NY 10158

Routledge is an imprint of the Taylor & Francis Group, an informa business

British Library Cataloguing-in-Publication Data
A catalogue record for this book is available from the British Library

Library of Congress Cataloging-in-Publication Data
Names: Harpham, Michael, author.
Title: Teamwork plain and simple : 5 key ingredients to team
success in schools / Michael Harpham.
Description: First Edition. | New York : Routledge, 2023. |
Includes bibliographical references and index.
Identifiers: LCCN 2022054562 (print) | LCCN 2022054563 (ebook) |
ISBN 9781032300870 (Hardback) | ISBN 9781032300887 (Paperback) |
ISBN 9781003303404 (eBook)
Subjects: LCSH: Group work in education. |
Teaching teams. | School management and organization.
Classification: LCC LB1032 .H374 023 (print) |
LCC LB1032 (ebook) | DDC 371.14—dc23/eng/20230120
LC record available at https://lccn.loc.gov/2022054562
LC ebook record available at https://lccn.loc.gov/2022054563

ISBN: 978-1-032-30087-0 (hbk)
ISBN: 978-1-032-30088-7 (pbk)
ISBN: 978-1-003-30340-4 (ebk)

DOI: 10.4324/9781003303404

Typeset in Melior
by Newgen Publishing UK

MIX
Paper | Supporting
responsible forestry
FSC   FSC™ C013985
www.fsc.org

Printed in the United Kingdom
by Henry Ling Limited

Contents

Acknowledgements

This book draws on my experience of leading and coaching teams in schools for over 30 years in the UK and abroad. From the many talented and inspirational leaders I have met along the way, I have learnt much. Their actions and their words are all represented and encapsulated in this book.

This book in particular draws on the study I completed for my doctoral research into factors influencing teams in schools. Heartfelt thanks to Greenwich University and, in particular, Professor Paul Miller, Professor Gordon Ade-Ojo, and Dr Ashley Brett for guiding me so skilfully through that experience over three years and to the teams involved for providing the data that enabled me to carry out and complete that journey – they know who they are.

As it is often said, life is a journey, not a destination, enriched and occasionally influenced by our fellow travellers. The creation of this book is no exception. Specific thanks must go to:

Annamarie Kino-Wylam, Molly Selby, Lauren Redhead, and Ting Baker at Routledge for their continued expertise in guiding me through the whole process a third time.

To Adrian Waters, Rosy Salam, Jon Meier and Aykut Kekilli for their helpful feedback.

Finally, to Julian, for his continued love, patience, and steadfast support.

Heartfelt thanks to all.

At the time of writing, there is a situation between Russia and the Ukraine. At a concert I attended recently, before the concert began, the great conductor Adam Fischer said:

When I was a child, I remember as a seven-year-old the Russians invading Budapest and the hardship and fear of living in a bunker. No child should ever have to experience such things. Their life is in the playground, not in the bunker.

It was a timely reminder that, as teachers and school leaders, we are here to empower and educate young people, through learning, to successfully manage whatever trials and tribulations life may present them, with love and kindness.

This book is therefore dedicated to all the teachers and school leaders across the world who as a school community, as a team, support children to effectively overcome the daily challenges they face and transform into the young adults they have the potential to become.

Also, at the time of writing an historic moment has passed with the death of Queen Elizabeth II. It is fitting therefore to include here an observation by her of teamwork and leadership:

> I know of no single formula for success, but over the years I have observed that some attributes of leadership are universal and are often about finding ways of encouraging people to combine their efforts, their talents, their insights, their enthusiasm and their inspiration to work together.

That is teamwork – plain and simple.

London, September 2022

About the author

Dr Michael Harpham is a headteacher, author, and educational consultant. He is Director of School Leader Development Ltd, a consultancy based in London that specialises in training and coaching for school leaders and their teams. Michael's national and international consultancy work includes one-to-one and team coaching, writing, and delivering bespoke training for leaders and their teams as well as writing and lecturing at universities across the UK.

As an educator, Michael has 30 years teaching experience, 20 of those at senior leadership level, including headship, in a broad range of schools in London and the Home Counties. Michael has extensive educational and leadership experience to share.

In addition, he has a Bachelors' degree from the Royal Academy of Music, two master's degrees in leadership and management and educational research, and completed his doctoral research into factors influencing the effective teamwork of leadership teams. He is also a Fellow of the Chartered College of Teaching and as such can bring significant authority and ability to his work.

Teamwork Plain and Simple is Michael's third book with Routledge. He is the author of *Progress Plain and Simple: What Every Teacher Needs to Know about Improving Pupil Progress* (2020) and *The School Leader's Year* (2021).

To contact Michael regarding consultancy, guest speaking, or training services, email him at michael@schoolleaderdevelopment.com.

Introduction

1.1 Beginnings

When I was growing up in Yorkshire in the seventies, surrounded by a stable mix of family, school and friends, by no means did I (or anyone else for that matter!) predict for that young lad, studying at the Royal Academy of Music, gaining a doctorate, publishing three books and being a headteacher. What all those instances had in common was that my journey through life crossed paths with teachers or other adults in a teaching capacity that spotted and helped me to develop the potential they saw in me.

Almost 50 years later, I continue to passionately believe in the transformative role education can play in our lives, at whatever age and whatever stage we find ourselves. But as teachers or school leaders, we cannot usually do that work alone. Most of us, when at work, are part of a team. Some of those teams can be great teams – supportive, functional, and successful. Others, for whatever reason, less so.

I am guessing, like you, I have been part of some truly successful teams. For example, when I was a team leader, we enabled a student to secure a place at the University of Oxford – the first student to reach this level in the school's 60-year history. When working with teachers and school leaders, I often quote Durant (2006), and his writing on Aristotle, encouraging self-reflection and improvement in that 'we are what we repeatedly do. Excellence being not an act, but a habit', something that successful teams understand and apply. Conversely, I am also guessing, like you, I have been part of some unsuccessful teams. This led me to ask why? Why are some teams more successful at work than others? Why don't some teams get into good habits?

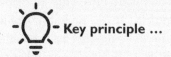

Key principle ...

Excellence is not just a one-off act, but a day-in, day-out habit.

DOI: 10.4324/9781003303404-1

So, if Aristotle is right (and at this point, 2300 years after he posited this notion, we have no reason to suspect otherwise!), and we are what we repeatedly do, as teachers and school leaders, as team leaders and team players, we need to repeatedly do the right things; right repeated individual actions will lead to successful individual behaviour, right repeated team actions will lead to successful team behaviour. This is succinctly coined in a phrase attributed to Henry Ford, who once said, 'if you always do what you've always done, you'll always get what you've always got'. To help less successful teams improve, something then is needed to break the cycle. Something needs to change.

 Key principle ...

As a team, or as a person if you always do what you've always done, you'll always get what you've always got.

What do successful teams do that unsuccessful teams do not? How do we know we are doing the right things if we have only been taught by poor teachers or led by poor leaders? How do we *know* that what we are doing is excellent? An answer as to why some teams are better at leading and managing themselves than others in the context in which they work may lie in the possibility that they understand what Descartes (1637) meant when he said, 'conquer yourself before you conquer the world'. In other words, improving and ensuring we have right individual intention and actions will lead to successful individual behaviour; improving and ensuring we have right team intention and actions will lead to successful team behaviour. Descartes' maxim therefore applies equally to the team as much as to the individual.

 Key principle ...

When looking to make a difference, conquer yourself before you go on to conquer the world.

So, what do successful teams do that unsuccessful teams do not? This question set in motion my doctoral study into teams, and its findings are at the heart of this book, providing five ingredients that are integral to effective and successful teamwork. But I did not just want my academic work to sit as a thesis on a university shelf gathering dust! Working in schools, and the pressures on the teams in those schools, means that more than ever before, there is a need to share this empirical research with professionals as well as academics.

As a result of reading this book, I hope you are closer to knowing that you are doing the right things as a team player or team leader. I hope after reading this book that you more effectively know what you as a team or team leader are doing well and what could be done differently. I hope in helping you identify the excellent individual/team habits you need for successful teamwork, where things are not going as well as they could be in the team, this book helps break that cycle, and in Descartes' words, helps the team conquer themselves, and by having more excellent team habits, your team can go on to conquer the world!

1.2 Aims of the book

This book is primarily written for teachers, support staff and leaders in schools who are working in or leading teams in those schools.

The first aim of this book is to clearly define what effective teamwork is – what effective teamwork looks like and how teamwork can be carried out more effectively in schools. The aim is also to suggest a model of effective teamwork in schools, based on empirical, proven research, and as a result, contribute to the discourse around school improvement – how we measure team success and what that means for teaching, learning and school leadership.

The second aim of the book is to support school teams and team leaders, to help them better understand how to be a more effective team and, as a result, help improve the leadership of schools and ultimately to improve school outcomes.

1.3 Why this book is needed

This book arises out of my 30 years' experience working in and leading various teams in schools and the doctoral research I carried out into leadership teamwork in schools. There are three reasons as to why this book is important: because teams in any organisation, in this case, schools, are important; because teams in schools are not working as well as they could be and because team leaders are not supported in their team leadership as well as they could be.

Teams in schools are important

The importance of teams in schools was heightened in the UK with the arrival of the Thatcher government (1979–1990) and their increased emphasis on the accountability of schools through the creation of performance tables and a government inspectorate – Ofsted (Gillard, 2018). This created greater pressure on the team leader to deliver success, which, as a result, was distributed through the formalisation and accountability of the leadership team at senior leadership level and the department team at middle leadership level. By the 2000s and the academisation of schools creating increased centralisation to that accountability (ibid.), this led to the team in schools being the central modus operandi by which schools deliver education, through which school leadership works and both schools and school leadership are judged today. In short, get teamwork right and you are more likely to get education right.

Teams in schools are not working as well as they could be

Second, schools in the UK are not working at the capacity at which they could be working. With around 80 per cent of schools judged as 'Good' or worse by the government's inspection arm, Ofsted (Ofsted, 2020) and 32 per cent of schools having a negative Progress 8 score according to the government's measure of expected progress in schools (DfE, 2021a), schools are not working to the capacity at which they are able. Hence the need to encourage and support more effective, and therefore more successful, teamwork and team leadership in schools. If schools are clearer about what effective teamwork looks like, there is a higher chance their results will improve and more schools are deemed successful. In addition, at present in the UK, teachers and school leaders on average are working approximately 57 hours a week, 60 per cent more than their European counterparts (Harpham, 2021). With more effective teamwork should come less individual unnecessary work for educators; schools working smarter, not harder.

Team leaders are not supported in their team leadership

Third, neither the government nor Ofsted provide any guidance or expectations to help support or guide the leadership of teamwork in schools.

Whether looking at the expectations of team leaders or the latest expectations of team leaders, senior and middle leaders as outlined through the National Professional Qualifications (NPQH, NPQSL and NPQML) (DfE 2021b), none of them inform or improve a leader's ability to develop and sustain teamwork, a further reason for this book. This book helps clarify for school leaders what the key ingredients of effective teamwork are and help ensure their team's work is therefore as effective as it can be.

1.4 How to use this book

This book is different from other books on leadership in being based on empirical research and focused primarily on school teamwork. It is also different in enabling individuals and teams to access the book and better understand teamwork and their team's work form an individual and collective perspective. There are examples and activities to do to help reflect on the teamwork in which you find yourself as well as tips and principles that underpin that leadership. These are indicated as follows:

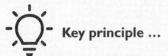

Key principle ...

Indicates a key principle underpinning teamwork that all teams must follow/be aware of.

Top tip ...

Indicates a top tip that can be applied to an individual or a group context to help improve the teamwork being practiced.

Team talk

Throughout the book there are moments when we need to pause and offer some practical examples of the key point in question. These are done in a 'Time out' style, pausing the narrative and offering a practical example as a 'Team talk'.

To ensure we are literally and metaphorically on the same page, we begin in Chapter 2 by clarifying what we mean by effective and successful teamwork. Chapter 3 explains how the five ingredients to teamwork came to be identified with Chapters 4 to 8 exploring each ingredient to teamwork in more detail and providing a useful audit to help you identify the extent to which that ingredient to teamwork is in place within your own team. Chapter 9 presents the key points emerging from research related to teamwork in an A–Z format for ease of navigation with a robust bibliography to help identify key research and literature which you may be interested in reading further.

Enjoy!

2 Defining teamwork

In this chapter we unpack:

▦ General and more specific definitions of teamwork

▦ The importance of being effective to be successful

▦ Team leadership and followership

▦ Team dynamics

2.1 Defining teamwork: what we mean by effective teamwork

The *Oxford English Dictionary* (2009) defines 'team' as a set of people working together, with 'teamwork' being the combined effort, or cooperation, of that team.

However, to help better understand how to recognise great teamwork and why it is great, and improve teamwork when it is not so great, we need a more detailed definition. In my research, this was provided by Kozlowski et al. (2009), who in their meta-analysis of 12 studies into work groups and teams defined a team as (a) two or more individuals who (b) socially interact (face-to-face or, increasingly, virtually); (c) possess one or more common goals; (d) are brought together to perform organisationally relevant tasks; (e) exhibit interdependencies with respect to workflow, goals and outcomes; (f) have different roles and responsibilities; and (g) are together embedded in an encompassing organisational system, with boundaries and linkages to the broader system context and task environment. Kozlowski et al. provide a succinct and useful working definition of the team – which I will use here – that a team is a collection of 'complex dynamic systems that exist in a context, develop as members, interact over time, and evolve and adapt as situational demands unfold' (Kozlowski et al., 2009, p. 116).

Rather than individuals working on the same task separately, teams are increasingly viewed as able to accomplish far more and elicit greater support for their

DOI: 10.4324/9781003303404-2

work than as individuals, with teamwork gaining acceptance for focused tasks and projects and being the major, sometimes only, emotional support in the school for team members. Furthermore, teamwork through synergy is viewed as essential to realise high performance, where both parties get something more out of the relationship than is expected and, as Covey (2020) indicates, is a habit of highly effective people and teams. Thus, teamwork can have a positive effect on project performance and therefore the school than would otherwise be the case.

The literature suggests that working together through interpersonal interaction is integral to the work of the team. Also, in the twenty-first century, team members are increasingly found in multiple locations, are culturally increasingly different and make increasing use of technology, individually and collectively, for example, the use of Google Classrooms, to accomplish work that is expected to be at a higher standard than ever before. This adds a small but relevant dimension to the quote from Kozlowski et al. (2009, p. 116) that the team is a 'collection of complex dynamic systems that exist in a context, develop as members, interact over time, and evolve and adapt as the situational demands *of the school* unfold'.

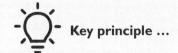 **Key principle ...**

The team is a collection of complex dynamic systems that exist in a context, develop as members, interact over time, and evolve and adapt as the situational demands of the school unfold.

In most Organisation for Economic Co-operation and Development (OECD) countries, teams perform tasks delegated by the team leader. However, what is delegated is managerial in scope, meeting the organisational needs of the school, rather than leadership and setting, influencing and shaping the work of the school. Team leaders hold significant responsibility in schools, not least for their contribution to the decisions made in running a school. They also ensure that the teaching and learning needs of the school are met; allocate resources where needed; hire and manage staff; keep the school running; and ensure the students achieve their expected results. In addition, they lead the school beyond the school's borders and through inter-school collaboration. In summary, team leaders are the bridge between the strategic 'head' leading the functioning 'body' of staff and ensuring both operate and function effectively. This may be interpreted as the ability of team leaders to manage the school to successfully operate within the fixed financial and statutory limits imposed upon it. A key function of team leaders therefore is as a conduit between the team leader and the staff. This adds further detail to Kozlowski et al.'s definition (2009) in providing the 'context' of the team, in being the bridge between the team leader and the rest of the school staff.

2.2 Defining teamwork: the link between effective and successful teamwork

The terms 'successful' and 'effective' in the literature have occasionally been perceived to be interchangeable, when in fact their meanings are very different. In terms of team leadership, both these terms are aiming to secure the same goal: that of every student achieving their potential and succeeding in their studies, which may explain why some feel the terms are interchangeable. However, Mestry (2016) clarifies the difference between 'successful' and 'effective' succinctly and clearly: successful teamwork or leadership has already been proven; it is a fact that it is successful by having previous actions that have *made* a positive difference and achieved success. Effectiveness can be viewed as the outcome of effecting a process, something *can make* a positive difference, resulting in success (ibid.); effectiveness therefore must occur *a priori* success.

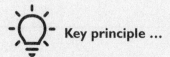 **Key principle ...**

Effectiveness leads to success. Only that which is effective can lead to success.

Furthermore, success can be ascribed to a one-off event, for example, success in an exam. However, an effective exam technique, which could be demonstrated in one exam, needs further additional exam success to be perceived as an established effective technique. Applying this to teamwork and team leadership means that, like one swallow not making a summer, while the work of a team successfully achieving one set of pupil outcomes means they are successful; the effective work or leadership of a team requires the process to be repeated, so that the team's work repeatedly leads to success (ibid.), and both the teamwork and the leadership of that team can be viewed as effective.

Within the literature for teamwork to be an effective process, Hall (2002) emphasised a capability to work together interdependently and maintain personal wellbeing between the team members. To facilitate this requires a compelling purpose, an appropriate group composition, a clear task structure and an agreement on core norms. According to New Leaders for New Schools (Martorell et al., 2010), six areas of responsibility defined effective teamwork or team leadership, five of which concurred with the Wallace Foundation's recommendations from their national empirical research (Mitgang, 2012). Successful teamwork or team leadership can therefore be viewed as *shaping a vision of success* for the school (and therefore the team); *creating a positive climate for education to flourish*; *cultivating leadership in others*; *improving teaching and learning*; and *managing school improvement*. The area not included by the Wallace Foundation was that of setting the *school culture.* Yet, Mitchell and Sackney (2000), Dering et al. (2006) and Parker (2008) all concur that the culture of a school and the norms that affect the success of that school are also rooted in the effective work of the team and team leader. This is summarised in the flowchart below with the team leader setting the framework for the team's work and school success.

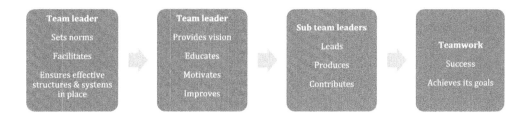

Not only does being successful follow being effective., being effective can only be ascribed following a number of successful demonstrations of that effectiveness. As illustrated above, the effectiveness of the team is predicated on the effectiveness of the team leader. It is a very rare team that can be effective without being effectively led. More on this later. However, in a school setting, the process outlined above must work within a set of fixed parameters. For example, the fixed number of staff (staffing) with set roles and responsibilities (workload), who need to deliver a prescribed curriculum (the national curriculum), through a set weekly or fortnightly timetable (fixed annual timetable), over a certain time frame (365 days a year, or 190 working days), in a set space (the school), with fixed resources (annual budget) to a set number of pupils (Pupil Admission Number) who need to demonstrate they have sufficiently learnt the curriculum (grade descriptors) and achieve a prescribed grade in standardised national tests by a specific date (results).

For the work of teams in schools to be successful, they must effectively deliver against each of these parameters (for example, by delivering within budget, a team may be regarded as effective). In essence, their effectiveness can be measured by the extent to which these parameters are experienced by the teams and the extent to which the school ultimately successfully achieves its goals within them.

In short, with so much in the team's world that is fixed, factors that detract from the curriculum being sufficiently taught on schedule and risk failure, may be regarded as factors that have a negative influence. As most, if not all, of us have experienced, managing the school's work in the face of a pandemic may be viewed as one such influence. Conversely, factors that ensure the curriculum is sufficiently taught on schedule and secures success may be regarded as factors that have a positive influence. Effective teamwork and team leadership leading to school success may therefore also be viewed as the team leader effectively managing to minimise any negative influences and promoting the positive influences within their work.

2.3 Defining teamwork: team leadership

In exploring the factors influencing effective teamwork in schools, the teams, their context, how they are led and how they respond to that leadership are all central to that exploration. At this point, I want to provide a better understanding of the theory behind teamwork, the dynamics within the team and the leadership of the team. What follows is a brief exploration of the key relevant theories in relation to the team leader, the team and the tasks and situation in which they work.

There are 'almost as many different definitions of leadership as there are people who have tried to define it' (Northouse, 2016, p. 2), with as many as 65 different classifications of leadership theory over the past 60 years. Of the 16 key theories related to leadership that were explored in detail, 11 are related in some way to team leadership. Of these 11, 3 are indirectly relevant, 4 are moderately relevant and 4 are directly relevant. For comprehensiveness here, the three theories that have low relevance and hence are not included, are trait theory, followership theory and adaptive leadership theory.

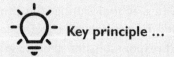

Key principle ...

Leadership has no single, clear definition applicable to every type of leader and every type of leadership.

The four theories that are moderately relevant are distributed leadership, Tannenbaum and Schmidt's continuum of leadership theory, shared leadership theory and transformational leadership.

Distributed leadership is moderately relevant as it is related to team practice but is controversial in that it is not always inherently good; Tannenbaum and Schmidt's continuum of leadership theory is also moderately relevant because I am interested to ascertain the different ways a team leader chooses to lead (and the consequent level of autonomy or freedom of the team) in response to the task or situation; shared leadership theory is similarly moderately relevant because I am interested in exploring to what extent members of the team are empowered to lead. Finally, I chose to engage with transformational leadership because it is an important leadership theory, and I am writing about the 'leader's ability to engage with others and create a connection that raises the level of motivation of both the leader and the follower' (Northouse, 2016, p. 162). However, while this theory may be useful for developing leadership teams and may be an influence on their effective teamwork, it is limited in its scope, focusing solely on the interaction within the team.

I am keen to explore three theories in more detail as they are all relevant, related to the factors influencing the effective work of the team and could potentially help us identify general patterns and focus. These are team theory, contingency theory and functional leadership theory because I am exploring the intrinsic and extrinsic factors affecting the team's work. Moreover, I am interested in a fourth theory, the models of motivation theory since the book is exploring the factors that affect the team's motivation. Below I outline each of these theories.

Team leadership theory espouses a different type of leadership compared to other theories, whereby 'the leader's job is to monitor the team and then take whatever action is necessary to ensure team effectiveness' (Northouse, 2016, p. 366). Thus, the leadership is located within the team and differentiates it from other styles of leadership, for example, Tannenbaum and Schmidt's continuum of leadership theory, where the leader is considered separate to the team. This theory proposes the idea that, for the leader, the balance of power (factor) determines (influences) how best to lead. Other key models of team leadership include the Hill model of team leadership, as well as descriptors of team effectiveness, for example, by Larson and LaFasto (1989) and Hackman (2012). The benefit of having such models includes that they are designed to support real-life working groups and provide 'a cognitive guide that helps leaders to design and maintain effective teams' (Northouse, 2016, p. 383). Critics of such models cite a lack of comprehensiveness in the identified leadership skills to be employed by the team and the assumption of team stability within a real world where teams have a 25 per cent turnover each year and are therefore far from stable.

The second theory of direct relevance here is linked to the contingency theory of leadership, which emphasises that the effectiveness of leadership is contingent on matching the leader's style to the internal or external situation. This is very similar to its more modern-day progeny, situational leadership theory, which 'provides a model that suggests to leaders how they should behave based on the demands of a particular situation' (Northouse, 2016, p. 112). Both these theories present the notion that it is the leader's response to the task or situation in relation to the needs of the team (factor) that determines (influence) how and who is best to lead. Critics of both situational and contingency theory expound that there is not a strong body of research to 'justify and support the theoretical underpinning' (Northouse, 2016, p. 112) and as such they lack clarity and validity, and fail to address key issues.

A third theory relevant here is functional leadership theory, which identifies the behaviours of a successful leader. Adair (1973) proposed in his action-centred leadership model that the leader should maintain a balance of concern for the individual, the task and the team. Later, Hackman and Walton's work (1986) identified the conditions for group effectiveness and how the team leader can facilitate this, with Zaccaro et al. (2001) emphasising a focus on team processes to secure improved team effectiveness. These theoretical models proposed that it is the leader's responsiveness to the team in relation to the task (factor) that determines (influence) how best to lead.

Finally, Maslow's hierarchy of needs (1943), Herzberg's two-factor theory (1959) and Vroom's expectancy theory (1964) are all examples of intrinsic or extrinsic theoretical models of motivation. First conceived in 1943, Maslow proposed a set of stages through which individuals are increasingly motivated in their work. Because a team is a collection of individuals, this hierarchy of needs could also be applied to a team. These needs include physiological needs, ensuring the team has good working conditions; the need for safety, ensuring the team feel and are safe and secure; social needs, ensuring the team have a sense of belonging, are accepting of each other socially; the need for esteem, have respect for each other, have status and recognition and self-actualisation; and the need to fulfil their own development and deliver.

The table below summarises these team leadership theories, which help sharpen the focus of the work in this book: how the leadership team works as a team and what determines how they are led.

Relevance	Theory	Determinant factor	Relevant research
Low	Trait Theory	Personality determines how the team is led	Eysenck, 1966; Myers, 1978; Kenny and Zaccaro, 1983; Lord et al., 1982; Mehra et al., 2006; Owens, 2006; DeRue et al., 2011; Harangus, 2011; Hoy and Miskel, 2012; Buble et al., 2014.
Low	Followership Theory	The symbiotic roles of leader and follower determine how the team is led	Bales, 1950; Lord, Foti, and Phillips, 1982; Kelley, 1988; Meindl, 1995.
Low	Adaptive Leadership Theory	The necessity for change determines how the team is led	Heifetz et al., 2009; Buble et al., 2014; Hallinger, 2016; Clarke and O' Donoghue, 2017.
Moderate	Distributed Leadership Theory	The workload determines how the team is led	Harris, 2004; Harris et al., 2007; Bush et al., 2012; Spillane, 2012; Tian, Risku and Collin, 2016.
Moderate	Continuum of Leadership Theory	Power/delegation determines how the team is led	Tannenbaum and Schmidt, 2008.

Continued on next page

Relevance	Theory	Determinant factor	Relevant research
Moderate	Shared Leadership Theory	Collective responsibility determines how the team are led and what they do	Crowther et al., 2009; Murphy, 2005; Gronn, 2009; Hallinger, 2011.
Moderate	Transformational Leadership Theory	Motivation determines how the team could be different and better	Dionne et al., 2004; Leithwood, Aitken and Jantzi, 2006; Hallinger, 2011; Hoy and Miskel, 2012; Yukl, 2013; Wiyono, 2018; Eisenberg et al., 2019.
High	Team Leadership Theory	The team determine how they are led	Larson and LaFasto, 1989; Burke et al., 2006; Kozlowski et al., 2009; Zaccaro et al., 2008; Morgeson et al., 2010; Hackman, 2012; Kogler-Hill, 2016.
High	Contingency Leadership Theory	The task/situation determines how the team is led	Fiedler, 1967; Hersey and Blanchard, 1969.
High	Functional Leadership Theory	Team behaviour in relation to task determines how the team is led	Adair, 1973; Hackman and Walton, 1986; Zaccaro et al., 2001; Hackman, 2002; Barnett and McCormick, 2016; Kouzes and Pozner, 2017.
High	Models of Motivation	The team's needs determine how they are led	Maslow, 1943; Herzberg, 1959; Vroom, 1964; Lawler, 1973; Argyris, 1974; Cranston and Ehrich, 2009; Buble, 2014.

2.4 Defining teamwork: team dynamics

In seeking to understand and present the theoretical aspects more clearly, this section outlines the theoretical constructs, variables, propositions, processes and assumptions that exist in the field and my research within it. My initial attempt to theorise the dynamics within a team drew on the theories of Herzberg (1959) and his two-factor motivational theory, Adair (1973) and his work on action centred leadership, Pastor, Meindl and Mayo (2002) and their work on social network analysis, and Belbin (2010) and his work on roles within teams.

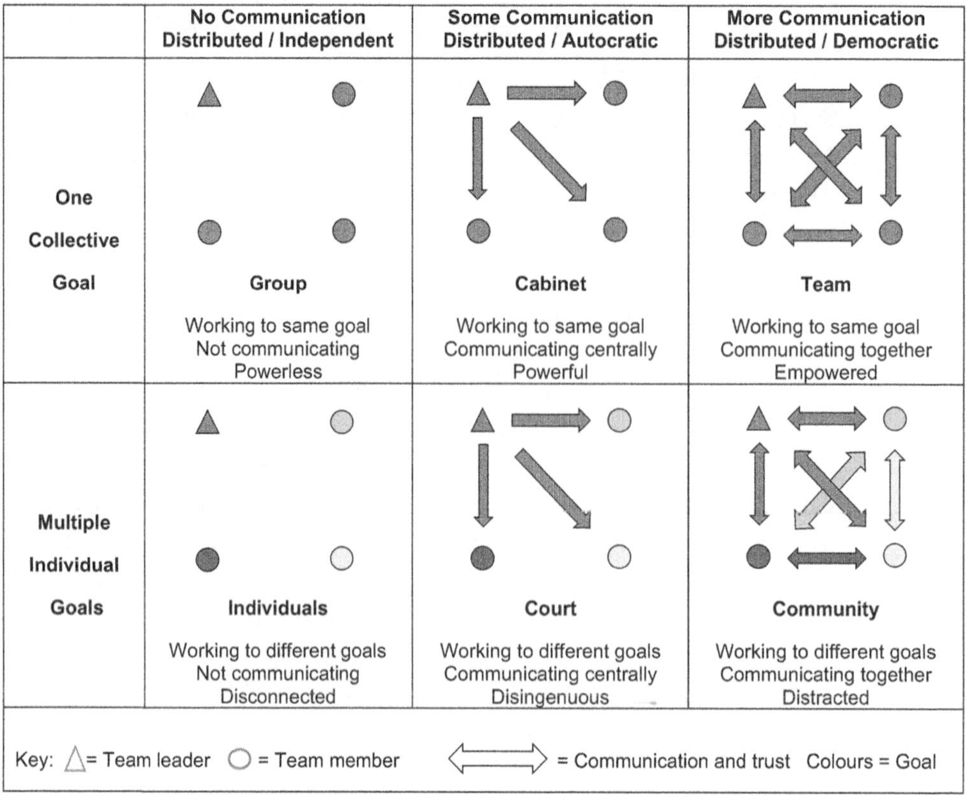

	No Communication Distributed / Independent	Some Communication Distributed / Autocratic	More Communication Distributed / Democratic
One Collective Goal	**Group** Working to same goal Not communicating Powerless	**Cabinet** Working to same goal Communicating centrally Powerful	**Team** Working to same goal Communicating together Empowered
Multiple Individual Goals	**Individuals** Working to different goals Not communicating Disconnected	**Court** Working to different goals Communicating centrally Disingenuous	**Community** Working to different goals Communicating together Distracted

Key: △ = Team leader ○ = Team member ⟷ = Communication and trust Colours = Goal

Figure 2.1 Team dynamics: conceptual framework – version 1

My conceptual framework is presented below as a summary of the different possible configurations of interactions within a team. I incorporated the people (team members) as circles, the team leader (as a triangle), their interactions (one-way as a single-headed arrow, two-way interactions as a double-headed arrow) and possible factors that affected them (goals as colours or communication as the number of interactions). This allowed for several representations of the differing dynamics within the team to be drawn. The diagram below illustrates the dynamics within the team in relation to goals (a single goal, or multiple goals) and power (laissez-faire, distributed leadership, allowing the team to be independent; autocratic, distributed leadership, requiring the team to follow communication from the centre; and more democratic, distributed leadership allowing the team to work together and potentially be empowered).

While this initial model enabled me to draw together the different internal relational influences between participants on the team (e.g. court or cabinet, with power being located with and distributed from the team leader) and to specify more clearly the differences between them, it did not facilitate additional external factors that may influence a team, such as Department for Education (DfE) directives. In addition, though this theoretical model considers the internal interactions

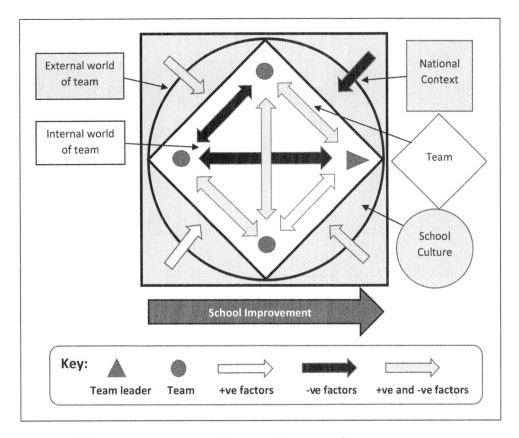

Figure 2.2 Team dynamics: conceptual framework – version 2

within the team and two external factors (communication and goals), it does not illustrate the positivity or negativity of an influence and the degree to which that influence is experienced. As Robson and McCartan (2016, p. 69) state, 'You won't get it right first time.' Thus, a refinement to the model was needed.

In developing my initial attempt to conceptualise the dynamics within a team, I revised this and synthesised the six different models to one representation of the interactions between the individual team members to more clearly represent the theoretical framework, through the internal (Herzberg, Hill, Adair and Belbin) and external (Herzberg, Hill, Adair and Fiedler) factors that affect the team's teamwork; the possible mono-directional influence of the individual, the task and the team on effective teamwork or the potential duo-directional influence of the different roles within the team; and the motivating, positive influence and / or demotivating, negative influential factors on their teamwork.

Drawing on their theories, the diagram above more closely represents the conceptual framework with which I am seeking to work in this book, in representing a team with multiple internal and external factors influencing it. The participants within the team (white square) interact together (two-headed arrow between team

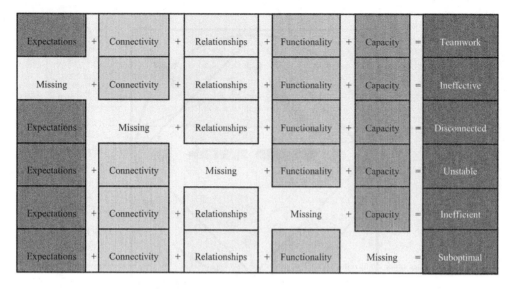

Expectations	+	Connectivity	+	Relationships	+	Functionality	+	Capacity	= Teamwork
Missing	+	Connectivity	+	Relationships	+	Functionality	+	Capacity	= Ineffective
Expectations		Missing	+	Relationships	+	Functionality	+	Capacity	= Disconnected
Expectations	+	Connectivity		Missing	+	Functionality	+	Capacity	= Unstable
Expectations	+	Connectivity	+	Relationships		Missing	+	Capacity	= Inefficient
Expectations	+	Connectivity	+	Relationships	+	Functionality		Missing	= Suboptimal

Figure 2.3 Team dynamics: a diagnostic model

members, and between team members and the team leader). These interactions may be either positive (white), negative (black) or a combination of both positive and negative (grey) in influence. The external factors of the national context and school culture may be neutral in influence (shaded grey) but also may be able to initiate positive influences (white arrow, upwards to the right, illustrating improvement), negative influences (black arrow, downwards to the left, illustrating regression) and both positive and negative influences on the team, depending how they are managed (grey arrow, progressing or regressing school improvement).

The above theoretical model, using arrows to depict the factors that influence the team illustrates the 'key factors, constructs or variables'. These key factors (arrows) can be mono-directional (single-headed arrows) or duo-directional (double-headed arrows) with either a positive (white), negative (black) or both positive and negative (grey) influence.

This theoretical structure moves Herzberg's two-factor motivational theory forward in that, yes, at work there are motivating and demotivating factors, but those factors may be solely positive (e.g. trust within the team) to be encouraged, solely negative (e.g. subversion within the team) to be discouraged and may be *both* positive and negative (e.g. expertise within the team) which needs to be managed.

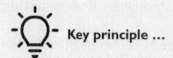 **Key principle ...**

Factors influencing the team may be solely positive, to be encouraged, solely negative to be discouraged and be both positive and negative, which needs to be managed.

Following my doctoral research, I returned to my motivation for embarking on it, to better understand why some teams in which I had worked were so successful and why some, despite seemingly best efforts, never seemed to quite achieve their aims. Analysing the patterns of the factors identified and their influence, it was clear that where teamwork went well, factors with a positive influence were present (e.g. trust). Where teamwork went less well, this was due to factors with a negative influence being present or with a combination of both positive and negative influences being effectively (or less effectively) managed, whether inside or outside the team. From the research findings, the diagram below offers a new diagnostic model for teams to ascertain the quality of their teamwork.

To explain the above diagram in a little more detail, if high expectations are present in the team's work, there are clear measures of success. Without these, progress may be insufficient or partial and, as a result, the team's work is not as effective as it could be.

Second, individuals within the team need to connect and interact in their work through, for example, communication or collaboration. Where this is not the case, it risks the team being disconnected and team members and their work becoming isolated.

Third, ensuring relationships are as conducive as they can be, provides the team with a happy, stable working environment. Where enmity and mistrust pervade, team members are likely to leave and hence create instability.

Fourth, within the team there must be an infrastructure that enables its work to function unimpeded. Without this, there is a risk that the work is not completed as consistently or as efficiently as it could be and thus leads to team inefficiencies.

Finally, the team having the capacity to complete its work within the given space, budget, resourcing and timeframe ensures the team's work is optimal.

Applying this diagnostic model to ascertain the strengths and areas for further development within a team enables them to clarify and engender a better understanding of how to improve teamwork, reduce individual workload, improve collective effectiveness and, consequently, secure increased school improvement.

By applying this diagnostic, those using it can improve teamwork in their own schools and thereby increase the improvement and collective success any internal or external accountability may require.

3 Five key ingredients of effective teamwork

In this chapter we unpack:

■ The five key ingredients to teamwork and explain why they are key

■ How the five key ingredients are connected

■ What happens when each ingredient is missing from the team's work

■ The teamwork diagnostic model and how to use it

3.1 Introduction

When studying teamwork in schools through the research I carried out, the data suggested 45 different factors that influenced teams and their work, positively, negatively and both positively and negatively.

From outside the school, the factors with a negative influence on teams, to a lesser or greater extent, included the government, COVID-19, and funding; smaller, both positive and negative influences included the experience of Ofsted, maintaining the school roll, links to industry, LEAs, and the need to perform and keep pace with competitor schools.

From within the school, the three largest factors with both a positive and negative influence are the students, other staff, and the team's workload. Other smaller factors that influenced the work of the teams both positively and negatively included parents, governors, and middle leaders; the vision and strategy for the school; the legacy the team inherited; and the safeguarding and structures in place (or not!).

The largest, predominantly positive, influences from the accepted behaviours within the school included having high expectations, supporting each other, and aligning with the school's ethos or culture. Positive team factors, but smaller in

DOI: 10.4324/9781003303404-3

influence, included holding each other to account, teaching, doing duties, being professional, being respectful, consulting, being innovative and developing in one's role.

The fly in the ointment was the negative school norm of a small number of staff being subversive.

Within the team, major, predominantly positive, factors influencing the team included the expertise and experience within the team, the leadership of the team leader, and the roles each team member fulfilled. Other smaller, mostly positive, influences within the team that were appreciated included the personalities within the team, the ability of the team to deliver, and the ability to trust each other.

Team norms, which also positively influenced the team, included, to a large extent, the sense of working together and communicating as a team. Smaller, positive influences included the way meetings were conducted, decisions were made, and targets were met, as well as how much the team were open and collaborative. A slightly less positive influence was how, in some schools, they occasionally worked in a state of emergency.

When considering the influences by size, the largest by far were from within the school (staff and students), with the government making its presence felt from outside the school, and the team's expertise and experience from within helping teams drive forward school improvement.

When looking for patterns and themes, my research (in brackets below) related closely with other researchers (Morgeson et al., 2010, p. 10), and their 15-point framework of team leadership functions, and, to a large extent, provides empirical support for their theoretical proposal (Barnett and McCormick, 2012). These patterns comprise:

Team expectations: 'Compose Team' (Roles, Personalities), 'Define Mission' (Vision and Strategy), 'Establish Expectations and Goals' (Targets, Ethos, Expectations), 'Monitor Team' (Accountability), 'Manage Team Boundaries' (Expectations), 'Challenge Team' (Accountability), and 'Perform Team Task' (Deliver, Performance).

Team interaction: 'Provide Feedback' (Consultation), 'Perform Team Task' (Collaboration, Communication), and 'Solve Problems' (Decision-making, Legacy).

Team behaviours: 'Solve Problems' (Subversion) and 'Support Social Climate' (Support, Trust, Openness, Respect).

Team infrastructure: 'Structure and Plan' (Structures), 'Provide Feedback' (Meetings), 'Monitor Team' (Meetings), and 'Manage Team Boundaries' (Leadership).

Team provision: 'Train and Develop Team' (CPD), 'Solve Problems' (Innovation), and 'Provide Resources' (Expertise, Funding).

These patterns and themes are summarised in the table below and explored further in the next section.

Patterns	Expectations	Interactions	Behaviours	Infrastructure	Provision
Theme	**progress**	**Connectivity**	**Relationships**	**Functionality**	**Capacity**
Influence	Meeting/ not meeting expectations	Increase/decrease in interactions	Helpful/unhelpful behaviours	Functional/ dysfunctional systems and infrastructure	Increase/decrease available provision
Impact	Increase/decrease in team success, progress & reputation	Increase/ decrease in team connectivity/ effectiveness	Increase/ decrease in positive team relationships	Increase/decrease in school/team functionality	Increase/decrease in team capacity and ability to deliver expectations and progress
Factors	Accountability	Collaboration	Cohesion	COVID-19	CPD
	Delivery	Communication	Openness	Decisions	Expertise
	Ethos	Consultation	Personalities	Duties	Finances
	Expectations	Competition	Professionalism	Emergency	Innovation
	Performance	Government	Respect	Leadership	School Roll
	Roles	Governors	Subversion	Legacy	
	Safeguarding	Home	Support	Meetings	
	Targets	Industry	Trust	Structures	
	Vision/Strategy	LEAs		Teaching	
		Middle Leaders		Workload	
		Ofsted			
		Parents			
		Staff			
		Students			

3.2 The five key ingredients to teamwork

In applying the summary of themes from my research into the real world, the following table will help distil how the five ingredients work together:

Key ingredient	Action by each team member	Action by the team
Expectations	What we are expected to do	What we are expected to do together
Interactions	What we do	What we do together
Behaviours	What we repeatedly do	What we repeatedly do together

Continued on next page

Key ingredient	Action by each team member	Action by the team
Infrastructure	How we organise what we (repeatedly) do	How we organise what we (repeatedly) do together
Capacity	How we support and improve what we (repeatedly) do	How we support and improve what we (repeatedly) do together

We begin our exploration of teamwork with what we expect to do individually as part of a team and as a team; is there clarity as to what we expect of ourselves individually and collectively? From those team expectations, we then need to look at how those expectations translate into our individual and collective actions; what we do individually and as a team. When these individual and collective interactions happen over time, they become individual and collective behaviours. However, with the evolution of these behaviours and the world around us ever changing, there is a need to review and ensure that what we repeatedly do together is as efficient and effective as possible, thus the need to organise a functional infrastructure that enables optimal teamwork to happen and be effectively supported and improved where necessary, so that that optima teamwork can be maintained over time.

 Key principle ...

For better or worse, the leadership, teaching, and learning in schools are the root cause of the progress, achievement, attainment, and success of those schools.

On a recent visit to Clos Lucé, Leonardo Da Vinci's final resting place, I was moved by the genius behind the models he created and one of the principles behind them, that 'movement is the cause of all life'. When applying this to our work in schools, this principle can be seen in our effectively educating the young people in our care so they achieve the qualifications they need to successfully move on to the next stage of their education or career. As an organisation, this principle can also be applied to schools in that the positive, constructive pieces of work made by each member of staff will help the school collectively successfully move forward together. To this end, it is incumbent on school leaders to facilitate this. Without sufficient movement made by the students in their learning as a result of the sufficient movement caused by the effective teaching from staff, students cannot successfully move on to the next phase of their education or career.

Thus, it is in our expectations that we identify the movement we wish to see happen; in our actions that we make that movement happen and in our interactions that movement happen with others; and through our behaviours that that movement happens repeatedly and consistently. Ensuring the infrastructure and capacity allow that movement to happen as effectively as it can, means our work as a team in schools with and for the students is as successful as it can be.

For team leaders, it is not only important to ensure the movement that is made by the team is sufficient but also that the connections between the team allow all movement made to continue unimpeded: it is not only the movement made by each member of staff but also the connections made between each member of staff that enables that movement to be made. Here in more detail are these ingredients.

Ingredient one: Team expectations.

Unifying theme: The expectations we have of ourselves and others help set the path towards team and whole school progress and success.

Measure of success: Meeting/not meeting expectations.

Influence on the team: Having expectations of ourselves and others helps us clearly understand as a team and as a school what we expect to see happen and, as a result, make the sufficient progress we need to make in successfully achieving our goals.

Without team expectations: There is no clear measure of success to our work and therefore we are unclear as to what is effective/ineffective or successful/unsuccessful. Without clear expectations, our work will not be as effective and therefore as successful as it could be.

Student success is the one measure by which schools most often stand or fall. Nine of the factors in my research can all be viewed under the umbrella of setting or maintaining (high) expectations. These comprise accountability (meeting our expectations), delivery (delivering what we expect to be delivered), ethos (what we expect to see in our school), expectations, performance (what others expect of us), roles (what the organisation expects of us), safeguarding (what the law expects of us), targets (the standard we are expected to reach) and the vision/strategy of the school (the goal we are expecting to reach). Their influence on the team is on helping them meet these expectations, the impact being to therefore achieve the school's aims and objectives. Hence, in setting and maintaining these expectations, they provide the milestones to the destination – the school ultimately fulfilling its potential, student success. As such, these factors are intrinsically related to the main key theme of progress.

Thus, the first key ingredient to team success are the high expectations we have of ourselves and others.

Ingredient two: Team interactions.

Unifying theme: The interactions we have between ourselves and others, help connect us together.

Measure of success: The degree to which we are connected/disconnected as a team.

Influence on the team: The more (positive) interactions we have, the greater the collective understanding of our work and therefore the more effective our response can be as a result and vice versa.

Without team interactions: There is no clear collective understanding as to the team's work and therefore the team's work can be disjointed, ill-informed and, as a result, not as effective as it could be.

Within my research, 14 factors were able to be grouped under the heading of interactions, either how the team interacts and connects, such as communication, consultation, or collaboration, or with whom the team interacts, such as themselves, the staff, governors, and students. Such interaction enables the team to effectively connect with their stakeholders and create a communication flow that enables information to be as current as possible, which, in turn, informs and enables team decision-making to be as effective as possible.

Drawing on my professional experience of success, or lack of it, the clarity, comprehensiveness, and coherence of our interaction was critical to the team's success. Given that the terms 'team leader' or 'principal' are in almost every member of a team's title, it is imperative that the communication that is generated from the 'head' or 'principal' team is as clear, comprehensive, and coherent as possible to ensure they minimise the potential negative impact of any miscommunication, all of which is within the team's power to get right.

Thus, the second key ingredient to team success is in how well the team interact together, with themselves and others.

Ingredient three: Team behaviours.

Unifying theme: How we behave as a team.

Measure of success: The extent to which we work positively/negatively with ourselves and others.

Influence on the team: The more positive relationships there are within the team and with others outside the team means the team and others are more likely to be happy and enjoy working together.

Without team behaviours: There can be mistrust and instability as people are increasingly unhappy and choose to leave the team.

Within my research, eight of the factors were all connected in that they are behaviours that individuals demonstrate to the improvement or detriment of the team's work. These include the ability for each member of the team to be open, professional, supportive, respectful, trusting, and trustworthy with each other. All these aid the sense of camaraderie and team cohesion. Less helpful to the team is when a team member's ego or personality are put before the good of the team, or where team members behave in a way that is overtly or covertly subversive.

Reflecting on my professional experience, I highlight a particular strategy that has been helpful in this context and that resonates with the connectedness highlighted above. I embraced challenging or subversive staff, as they were usually either highly intelligent and felt they knew more or could do better, were creative thinkers that felt there was a better way to do something, or had ideas that were not being heard. Either way, being available to listen to and take on board their critique, helped make them feel a valued part of the team, turning them from subversive enemies to critical friends.

Thus, the team's behaviours can either increase or decrease their working relationships and consequently, positively or negatively influence the team's interactions and functionality, and as a result, the team's ability to deliver school improvement.

The third key ingredient to team success then are the positive relationships team members have, within the team and with others outside the team.

Ingredient four: Team infrastructure.

Unifying theme: The ability of the team to function and be functional.

Measure of success: The extent to which the team functions.

Influence on the team: The more effective processes and procedures the team have in place, the less reliant the team are on individuals, the team able to work like a well-oiled machine, as everyone knows what to do and when.

Without a team infrastructure: The team is likely to be inefficient, dysfunctional, and unlikely to successfully accomplish its work to the expected standard or given time frame.

For any interactions (communication) to be successful, the structures to facilitate that communication (infrastructure) must be in place and functioning effectively. A further ten factors can be grouped under the heading of how we work together as a team or as a school; the shared value being that all the factors are related to team or school functionality.

These comprise COVID-19 (ensuring the school functions safely in the current pandemic), decision-making and meetings (ensuring the best decisions are made to help the school reach optimal functionality), leadership, structures and legacy (ensuring the best decisions are made at the best time to enable the school to reach optimal functionality, despite or with the legacy inherited by the team), teaching (ensuring the school functions well in lesson time), duties (ensuring the school functions as well as it can outside of lessons), emergency (when the school does not function as well as it can), and workload (what this all means to the functionality of the team).

From my experience as a trainer and leadership coach, this area is the least understood and therefore the area most neglected in schools. When the team are less effective, job descriptions are left unrevised, meetings poorly managed, and leadership decisions ill-informed. Where they are more effective, the opposite is true.

The theme emerging from all these factors therefore is in the infrastructure of the school or the team and the influence of the factors in increasing the functionality or dysfunctionality of the team / organisation.

Thus, the fourth key ingredient to team success is in the infrastructures the team has in place that allow it to function well.

Ingredient five: Team provision.

Unifying theme: The capacity the team has to deliver on expectations and improve.

Measure of success: The ability to maintain/increase team capacity.

Influence on the team: Having the ability to provide for the needs of the team, enables the team to be self-sufficient and able to meet the changing/multiple demands it faces.

Without team capacity/provision: The work of the team is likely to be suboptimal, as the team are not as capable as they could/should be or are unable to meet the required expectations due to other demands taking them away from their essential work.

In my research, the final five factors influencing the team enabled them to do their work more effectively because of their presence rather than their absence. Thus, finances in the black and a full school roll enable the team to work unimpeded and being open to new ideas and having the right skills and development programmes in place all help the school improve more effectively. From this pattern of provision, one can ascertain the degree to which the team have the capacity to deliver on their expectations and progress. This position is conversant with the lessons I have taken from my own professional experience, whereby team development is the area that can have significant impact on team effectiveness in upskilling or increasing the knowledge of the team and raising the quality of the work they do.

Thus, the fifth key ingredient to team success is in its capacity to provide for the needs of the team and ensure it is able to successfully maintain/deliver the other four ingredients.

3.3 How the five key ingredients are connected

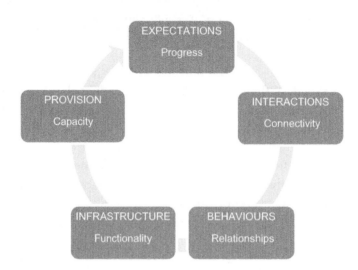

Figure 3.1 The 5 key ingredients to team success and how they connect

The figure above summarises the key ingredients and the order of priority. These include expectations and how these all help the team to deliver pupil progress; the pattern of interactions and how these support team connectivity; the team's behaviours and how these contribute to the team's relationships; the infrastructure within the school and the team facilitating team functionality; and how the provision available to the team aids their capacity to deliver school improvement.

1. **Set high expectations and build these into a plan.** Setting out clear, high expectations for the team to meet will help the team to be clear about their goal, how they each contribute to the achievement of that goal, and helps clarify how to be effective and clearly demonstrate progress. These expectations would be well placed in a school or faculty development plan. Everything then follows from that plan.

2. **Clarify the interactions that need to take place to ensure the right people are doing the right things at the right time and in the right way.** The plan needs to be a lived experience through the team. Connecting the team together clarifying who is responsible for completing what and when, will help the team interact and more effectively work together.

3. **Insist on positive relationships from the team.** The plan needs to be delivered, and the team are responsible for delivering it. Occasionally difficulties arise that need to be resolved. Developing helpful behaviours increases the positive relationships within the team and the stability of the team.

4. **Ensure the team's work is fully supported to succeed.** Creating systems, processes, and procedures helps the team function efficiently.

5. **Develop the capacity of the team.** This enables the teamwork to be optimal and increase in impact

3.4 What happens when each ingredient is missing from the team's work

To better understand why some teams are successful and why some never seem to quite achieve their aims, it was clear in my research that where teamwork went well, factors with a positive influence were present (e.g. trust) and where teamwork went less well was due to positive factors being poorly managed by the team or the team leader, or simply not present at all.

From the research findings, having unpacked the key ingredients to teamwork, it is now time to consider what happens when these ingredients are either not managed as well as they should be, or are not present.

First, if expectations are present in the team's work, there are some form of a measure of success in place. However, it is not only the presence of expectations that will lead to success. For them to be effective, they all need to be clear, SMART, and sufficiently high enough that in meeting them the team (and therefore the school) achieve their goals. In drawing on the earlier discussion where effectiveness leads to success, if expectations are not all present or all are not clear enough, smart enough or sufficiently high enough, being held to account against those expectations and delivering those expectations, the team will be less effective than

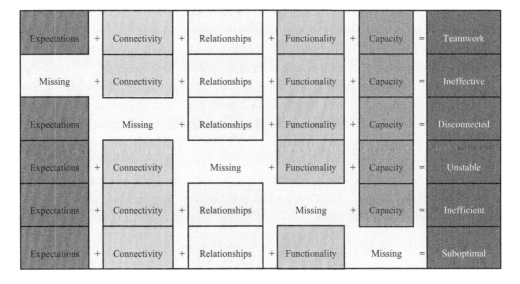

Figure 3.2 Team dynamics: a diagnostic model

they could be. Thus, where expectations are not sufficiently present, the team is more likely to be ineffective than they could be.

Second, the team need to connect and interact in their work, with themselves and others. When this is in place, the team communicate, collaborate, and consult between themselves and with others so that they are sufficiently connected and work as a complete unit within themselves and as a whole ecosystem with others. Where this interaction is not sufficiently or effectively in place, it risks members of the team being disconnected from the rest, or those outside the team who are important stakeholders in the team's work becoming isolated. Thus, where interactions are not sufficiently present, the team, and those connected to the team, are more likely to be disconnected from important work than they could be.

Third, by ensuring relationships are as conducive as they can be, provides the team with a happy, stable working environment. Where this is not the case, enmity and mistrust pervade, with team members more likely to leave and hence create instability. Therefore, ensuring that relationships within the team, and with others connected to the team are open, honest, professional, respectful, trusting, and supportive will lead to staff wanting to remain in position. When team members form cliques, are subversive, closed, dishonest, unprofessional, disrespectful, untrustworthy, or unsupportive, can lead to staff not wanting to remain in position and therefore leave. Thus, where relationships are not sufficiently present, the team, and those connected to the team, are more likely to be unstable and create instability, than they need to be.

Fourth, within the team there must be an infrastructure that enables its work to function unimpeded. Without this, there is a risk that the work is not completed as consistently or as efficiently as it could be and thus leading to team inefficiencies. For example, through poor decision-making through lack of consultation or too much discussion, poor leadership of the team, poor budget handling, historical poor decisions, poorly managed meetings, incoherent, or illogical staff structures, or poorly managed workload. Thus, where the team's infrastructure is not as robust as it could be, the work of the team, and those connected to the team, are more likely to be inefficient and therefore not as effective as they could be.

Finally, the team having the capacity to complete its work within the given space, budget, resourcing, and timeframe ensures the team's work is making best use of what it has at its disposal and therefore optimal. Thus, when training opportunities, individually or collectively, are not being effectively utilised, expertise within the team being effectively mobilised, available finances being put to efficient use and technology, new ideas or ways of working being explored, can lead to the team not working as effectively as it could be and the work of the team therefore being viewed as suboptimal.

3.5 The teamwork diagnostic model and how to use it

The following chapters provide a team audit against each of these five ingredients to support your team in diagnosing and ascertaining the strengths and areas for further development within the teamwork of your team. This should then enable you to clarify and better understanding how to improve your teamwork, reduce individual workload, improve collective effectiveness, and, consequently, secure increased team and school improvement.

It is my hope that by applying this diagnostic, those using it can improve teamwork in their own schools and thereby increase the improvement and collective success any internal or external accountability may require.

4 Key ingredient 1: clear expectations – clarifying team progress

Influence on the team: Helping meet expectations

Impact: Increasing team success and reputation

4.1 Team expectations: introduction

This chapter outlines in more detail what we mean by clear team expectations, the influence and impact on the team and others when expectations are clear and sufficiently high, and when our expectations are less clear or suboptimal. It unpacks in more detail the importance of having a clear vision and implementing a clear strategy with focused targets to achieve that vision. This is the first key ingredient because without having a clear goal in mind for the team and the strategy, and targets to achieve that goal, there is no teamwork and no team leadership. Steve Radcliffe sums it up succinctly with his 'Future – Engage – Deliver' – begin with the end in mind.

The rationale for these key takeaways in this order, is that to achieve our team's vision, we must ensure we have all the statutory requirements on our work covered, hence these are considered next. These are followed by ensuring that everyone within the team is working efficiently to achieve our goals through having clear roles and responsibilities. As with any journey, checking we are where we need to be at the right time, checking we have achieved and done what needs to be done to the quality and level to which is expected is considered next. This includes how we hold ourselves and the team effectively to account and agree, implement, and embed team expectations inherent within the team's ethos. Finally, teamwork in schools is never completed within a vacuum and so the next consideration for the team is that the expectations we have of ourselves are realistic. We must be clear about what is realistic and unrealistic in what we can deliver when dealing with the expected and the unexpected within our work.

DOI: 10.4324/9781003303404-4

4.2 Team expectations: audit

To clarify the extent to which your team or school's expectations are in place and working well, consider completing this short audit, either by yourself or with the rest of the team/school. Once completed, you will be able to identify the expectations that require immediate action (expectations that need to be in place/ need urgent revision); expectations that require short-term action (expectations that need tweaking/need to be more consistent), or that require medium-term action, identifying the team's/school's next steps.

Team expectations audit	Positive measure	In place working well	In place needs tweaking	In place needs work	Not in place	Negative measure
1-year plan	Measurable					Unmeasurable
3-year strategy	Achievable					Unachievable
Accountability	Robust					Absent
Expectations	Met					Not met
Job descriptions	Clear					Unclear
Responsibilities	Clear					Unclear
Safeguarding	Effective					Ineffective
Statutory requirements	Compliant					Non-compliant
Targets	High enough					Too high/low
Vision	Clear					Unclear

Follow up:
Immediate action (expectations need to be in place/need urgent revision):
Short-term action (need tweaking/need to be more consistent):
Medium-term action (identify next steps):

4.3 Team expectations: vision, strategy, and targets

The importance of having a powerful vision of the future is key to the success of any team or school. Everything that a team or school does should stem from that vision and feed into the achievement of that vision. To ensure any team can begin their journey with a firm step forward, here are a few pointers to set them off in the right direction.

Vision and strategy: have realistically ambitious goals

For any school it is important to have a clear goal in the future that is aiming for a realistic improvement compared to where they are now. That improved goal can come in many guises, but the key is for the goals set to be high but to also be attainable. I remember when applying for universities, my teacher at the time encouraging me to aim for the highest possible goal, in addition to the universities that were more attainable. To my surprise, I got into the top university (I fitted the bill in what they were looking for – something I would not have known when I applied). Thus, his point was a good one; always aim realistically high, you never know your luck! Similarly, a vision for the team must be ambitious, realistic, and clear, helping motivate the team and secure progress. If the goal is too ambitious, not ambitious enough, or too nebulous, it can be unachievable and demotivating for the team as a result of not making sufficient progress due to key milestones not being achieved.

Top tip ...

Set out a clear vision, strategy, and SMART targets that are ambitious, achievable, deliverable, and help the team be clear about future actions.

Vision and strategy: have short-term and long-term plans

When you take a step forward, how do you know it is in the right direction? Because you have a long-term goal that guides those short-term steps. Long-term plans (plans lasting 2–5 years) for teams and schools are useful because they give meaning and coherence to both short-term plans (longitudinal goals) and the multiple targets schools need to achieve (lateral goals). Thus, while everything a team or school does daily, feeds into the achievement (or otherwise) of its annual development plan, these annual improvements should feed into the achievement of its long-term plans. Even teams or schools working in challenging circumstances who suffer from high staff mobility for example, can benefit from having a long-term plan, giving shorter-term plans greater strategic coherence.

Key principle ...

The team/school with both short- and long-term plans are more likely to reach their long-term goal because they know where they are ultimately heading.

Vision and strategy: ensure your vision and strategy are comprehensive, coherent, and clear

Ensuring that the work the team does is the only work that needs to be done is a key skill for any leader. All team leaders are the recipients of scores of emails offering exciting new projects, involvement with the latest piece of research, or participation in a national or local initiative that offers exciting, high-profile experiences for staff and students. All this can seem exciting stuff; however, with any project, be it large or small, teams in schools have only a fixed amount of time, a fixed amount of energy, and a fixed amount of resources for us to get the job done; anything that takes that time, energy, or resources away from the necessary work that needs to be completed, needs to be resisted at all costs. Unless of course the team are on track to achieve their goals and there is time, energy, and resources to spare! Therefore, as a rule, always only do first that work that needs to be done.

In a similar way, ensuring the work of the team is structured coherently, completing a specific project first that helps build and put into place a key step on which subsequent work can build, is key to a team achieving its ultimate goals.

Finally, a strong, clear vision motivates and gives meaning to the work of a school. It enables the team to quickly understand and ensure everybody is focused on improvement. However, a strong, clear vision that is not necessarily practical, meaning more talk and less action, and where community/stakeholder misperceptions may exist, can pose significant challenges for the team. Thus, a clear plan enables more efficient delivery and speedier school success. An unfocused plan or a plan with multiple aims, means increased inefficiency, with the necessary work not getting done. This is especially true for long-term targets, which need clear, specific short-term milestones and the necessary time to implement them.

To aid the clarity of a vision and strategy, having a shared, collectively created vision means respecting differences and enables the collective buy-in from the team and the school, and vice versa. Having a clear vision means putting forward the right actions in the right order for people to carry out and complete. Not doing this means the team may not deliver the right things and therefore reduces confidence in the team. However, doing, or putting in the right order the things that need doing, means the team are more likely to deliver the right things for the school and therefore boost the confidence within the team.

 **Top tip ...**

With a comprehensive strategy, team time and energy are effectively used to achieve the team's goal; with a coherent strategy, steady, explicit team progress is made in achieving the team's goal; with a clear strategy, the speed with which the team are likely to deliver their goal increases.

Target setting

When setting targets, it important for the collective agreement of those targets by the team. Similarly, it is important to long-term plans for targets to be quantifiable and clear to aid the achievement of those targets.

Target setting: have SMART rather than unSMART targets

Using SMART targets is an age-old method for ensuring that when setting targets, they are as good as they can be. For school leaders that have not come across SMART targets, or need a refresher, a SMART target is:

	SMART target example	**UnSMART** target example
Specific	Achieve at least 75% ...	Aim to achieve a high number ...
Measurable	At least 95% of Year 10 students 'agree' or 'strongly agree' they feel safe	Students feel safe in school
Achievable	Present a detailed analysis of progress in pupil behaviour every month	Present a detailed analysis of progress in pupil behaviour each week
Realistic	Gather a sample of at least 5% of all stakeholder views on homework	Gather all stakeholder views on homework
Time-related	By the end of term complete ...	Complete ...

Target setting: keep targets clear and simple

A lack of targets, or unclear targets, mean a lack of focus for teamwork. This also applies when two targets are set (e.g. a quantitative and a qualitative target), which means two targets have to be reached, raising the number of targets to be achieved by the team and thus increasing team workload.

Where quantifiable, aspirational targets are achieved, the work completed by the team is sufficiently challenging, and to the standard it should be. Where aspirational or quantifiable targets were so aspirational that they are unachievable (e.g. 'We aim to be in the top 1% of schools in the country'), work can become too challenging and not completed to the expected standard. In addition, when targets are met, the team can feel a sense of achievement, whereas when targets are unmet, there can be a sense of disappointment.

The importance of having SMART targets also lies in the ability for team leaders to be able to effectively hold their team to account. Being held to account as a team against unSMART targets (for example, any of the above) means work completed may not meet expectations and be unfairly judged, creating unnecessary disharmony amongst the team.

Similarly, when expectations are unrealistic and risk being largely unmet, the team are not as effective as they could be and are likely to feel frustrated, diminishing credibility and reputation, whereas meeting ambitious but realistic expectations (e.g. 'Having been in the top 10% of school for 3 years, we aim this year to be in the top 5% of schools in the country'), gives the team a real sense of achievement.

 Top tip ...

To ensure the team are clear as to what needs to be achieved and to support accountability – have SMART targets.

Target setting: set targets with collective agreement

Collectively agreed targets give an increased sense of ownership to those targets, though this also usually means more highly challenging work for the team leader. One participant in my research commented:

> With the line management of departments, it's so important to have that overview of what's going on outside your own area of responsibility, so having that responsibility shared across the team and able to bring it all together I think has quite a positive influence because of that ownership.

Efficient target setting: longer term and online

Having targets that are set over a number of years means less work in creating new targets and setting new objectives. Similarly, using online data management systems means less work for the team, online systems being more accurate and more user-friendly.

4.4 Team expectations: statutory expectations/requirements on the team

Statutory expectations/requirements: review and update frequently

All of the statutory expectations/requirements below are drawn from guidance issued by the Department for Education. Central to the work of any school is that students are able learn in an environment that is safe and happy. As such, safeguarding is a legal necessity that must be in place for the school to be functioning within the law. Hence, when safeguarding issues occur, they are urgent, important, and must be handled properly.

Consequently, they can be a significant negative influence on the team. Indeed, in my research, work related to safeguarding was a high priority compared to other work and required a high level of team time when dealing with such issues. They created high pressure for the team in managing the issues and a sense of guilt in those who were not dealing with them. But it did mean the team ensured the school was a safe environment for students, enabling the school to function well.

Area	Statutory guidance
Administration and finance	Capital transactions
	Change of land use
	Home-to-school travel and transport
	Transport to education and training (16 and over)
	Financing schools
	Schools causing concern
	School uniform
Admissions	School admissions and appeals
Assessment	Assessment targets for SEN pupils
Behaviour and attendance	Alternative provision
	Behaviour and discipline: parents and governors
	Children missing education
	Suspensions and exclusions
Careers guidance	Participation of young people: education, employment, and training
	Careers guidance
Curriculum	The National Curriculum
Early Years Foundation Stage	Statutory framework
Governance	Constitution of Governing Bodies
	School Governance
Looked-after children	Designated teacher for looked-after children
	Children Act 1989
Safeguarding	Keeping Children Safe in Education
	Working together to safeguard children
	Multi-agency guidance on FGM
	Promoting the education of looked-after children
	Supervision of activity with children
	Children Act 1989

Continued on next page

Area	Statutory guidance
SEN	Education of SEN children who cannot attend school
	SEND Code of Practice
	Supporting students with medical needs
Staff employment and teachers pay	Induction of NQTs
	Initial Teach Training criteria
	School Teacher's Pay and Conditions

Top tip ...

Ensure the team are clear about the statutory expectations/requirements on the team, and that these are always evident and secure.

4.5 Team expectations: team roles and responsibilities

The first port of call after establishing the end goal/vision for the team is outlining what that means for each member of the team in reality. Clarifying each person's role/responsibilities through an up-to-date job description and staffing structure is key to ensuring everyone in the team is working efficiently and effectively.

Team roles and responsibilities: are in place and clear

Have you ever been in a situation where you expected someone else to be doing something, but they thought you were doing it instead, so neither of you did what needed to be done? Or when two people do something at the same time, meaning one of you has wasted precious time that could have been spent doing something more meaningful? In my experience of schools, work accountability and job completion issues can often be needlessly created when a person's job description is out-of-date, unclear, mismatched to the leader's abilities, or just not there! What bigger sign of value and respect can an employer show than to have a clear division of roles and responsibilities that match a person's strengths and areas of development? When these are disregarded and forgotten, especially regarding the clarity of roles encapsulated in the job description, can create unnecessary aggravation to the team's work. Having an up-to-date job description enables the team to use its time and energy efficiently, minimising work duplication and the assumption that someone else, somewhere else is doing the work. In addition, where a member of the team is absent for significant periods, there may be a knock-on effect for the rest of the team who are required to 'pick up the pieces' in their absence. When a clear job description is not in place, key work may not get done.

Team talk: who is responsible for managing pupil behaviour?

A perfect example of what we are discussing with regard to job descriptions and clarity over roles and responsibilities is with regard to managing pupil behaviour. When a student with SEN misbehaves repeatedly in a lesson, is it the Head of Department's responsibility to deal with it as the misbehaviour is occurring repeatedly in their department's lesson? Is it the Head of Year's responsibility, as the repeated misbehaviour is by a student in their year group? Or is it the SENDCO's responsibility as the student has a recognised educational need?

If job descriptions are not clear, each of the middle leaders specified above would be justified in assuming the misbehaviour was being picked up by someone else, leaving the misbehaviour to go unchecked. Being clear that in the first instance it is the Head of Department's responsibility to deal with it, as the repeated misbehaviour was in their subject's lessons (pattern = same lesson/same teacher and therefore a curriculum issue), in liaison with the Head of Year (there may be misbehaviour in other lessons, the pattern = multiple lessons/same pupil and therefore a pastoral issue), and the SENDCO (there may be misbehaviour in other lessons, the pattern = multiple lessons/same pupil and therefore an SEN issue).

Ensuring clarity over who is responsible for what, or who instigates a process/procedure, helps the team to work efficiently and effectively together.

It is clear that team roles and the expectations outlined within the job description are vital to the functionality of the team and a central part of the team's self-efficacy. They are thus essential to the performance of the school as well as key to job satisfaction. Thus, it is important to ensure that team roles and the expectations of the team are up to date, clear, and aligned to each team member's strengths.

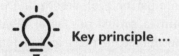 **Key principle ...**

Distributed leadership can only work when leaders are there.

Similarly, having an organisational chart in place, provides an overview as to the coherence of the structure of staffing in the school and allows everyone at a glance to see how the school works as a functioning organism. Indeed, clear, professional, constructive, and sufficiently high expectations mean staff can do well in their role, whereas unclear, too low, or too high expectations mean staff may not do well in their role.

As a result, a lack of clarity of the role can mean a lack of accountability and increased team workload as others pick up the pieces or duplicate work; conversely, clarity of the role means better accountability and decreased team workload. When the team fulfil their roles, it means important schoolwork gets done, including being critical with each other. When the team do not fulfil their roles, it means important work does not get done and the effective and efficient distribution of leadership does not work.

Top tip ...

Have clear, aligned job descriptions in place that minimise overlap between responsibilities and create clear personal accountability.

Team roles and responsibilities: maximise team strength through distributed leadership

Distributed leadership means everybody in the team does their share of the teamwork and gets the work done. It enables the team leader to get on with other things and the team to challenge each other, be respected, and have a sense of responsibility in their roles. Conversely, although it creates more effective leadership, it means more voices are around the table, taking up time in discussion rather than action. Furthermore, while it develops leadership, where there is a perceived hierarchy of roles, it means some roles can be viewed as subordinate and limits leadership. It also means that when anybody does not do their share of the work, it can be divisive for the team and creates more work for others. Thus, while distributing leadership and/or work within the team, this comes with a risk that it might not get done to the expected quantity or quality. This is why distributed leadership, while being a leadership panacea to developing capacity and getting more from a team, has a strong caveat in needing to be applied with discretion.

Similarly, there has been a tendency for team leaders to move people around in their roles to develop experience in areas additional to team member's expertise. Again, this should only be applied to team members who have the potential for reaching much further than they are, as keeping people with the right expertise in the right role maintains strong team delivery, whereas having people without expertise in the same role hinders team delivery. Moreover, moving roles around in the team in the long term is beneficial because it strengthens the team and means in the long term that the team are as much generalist as specialist. However, not rearranging roles in the short term can mean less anxiety and more confidence in the roles for the team members.

Having individuals in the right roles contributes well to schoolwork; however, having individuals in the wrong roles does not contribute well to schoolwork. In addition, when the team use their strengths in their roles, and the team work well in their roles together, the team can be more effective; however, using their strengths in their roles but not supporting others beyond this, or if there is a mismatch between a team member's personality and role, can reduce the team's effectiveness.

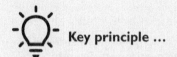

Key principle ...

Distributed leadership = distribution of the work but not the responsibility for that work.

4.6 Team expectations: team accountability

Accountability: mutual accountability is highly effective teamwork

Governors, the headteacher, and the team leader regularly hold teams to account, making teamwork more manageable and more effective through their challenge and support. When the team is not held to account and not doing what they should, and getting away with it, it is not helpful to the team, meaning additional workload for others. In addition, when the team has the expectation of holding each other to account it means more regular challenge for the team, is motivating and means work is done more effectively as a result. However, where there is an expectation that only the team leader can hold the team to account, less effective teamwork is done as a result. Similarly, communication from and being held to account by governors who are non-specialists can lead to misunderstandings within the team.

On the upside to mutual accountability in teamwork, the role of governors and the ability to work online in holding a team to account are all beneficial to teamwork. Having high expectations that the team use when holding each other to account also facilitates more effective teamwork.

Counter-intuitively, team accountability can be experienced less positively where there is excessive support from the team leader, smothering with care and support, but ultimately disabling effective accountability. Similarly, having non-specialists as governors who set targets that are unclear and not as SMART as they could be, can also add to the potential for ineffective accountability outside the team's control.

Team talk: Internal challenge = internal growth

Most schools now have accountability meetings with middle leaders to identify what is going well with pupil achievement and present an opportunity to share good practice, as well as what could be better and is an opportunity for staff training.

A good example of this was when we were looking at the data from different departments and trying to ascertain why there was such a disparity in final performance compared to department predictions.

A standard question to check the assessment procedure was 'how have the internal grades being arrived at?' The answer from one department was 'in line with policy, we do an average of all the assessments to date'. When another department was asked the same question, they answered 'we gave the latest assessment result' (antenna starts twitching). A third department responded with 'we had a great way of working in my last school, which we all really like, so our department give the grade we think the students will achieve at the end of the year' (antennae positively waving). After asking the same question to all Heads of Department, it was clear that the assessment policy was not being followed as rigorously or as consistently as it should have been, leading to the large disparity, not in the pupils' work, but in the teacher's assessment of that work.

Thus, it is key for any team to be clear on the measures of success and that the team ask those key questions that help shine a light on great practice to be shared but also on practice that needs to be improved and supported.

 Top tip ...

Have a balanced process of team accountability, which celebrates positive progress and strengthens areas of development.

4.7 Team expectations: team ethos

The team's ethos is the accepted norms within the team – it is how we do things round here. This can range from turning up to meetings punctually (or not), to emailing frequently and cc-ing everyone in. This section outlines and clarifies the importance of getting the team ethos right in supporting more effective teamwork.

Team ethos: ensure the department/school have a clear team ethos

All researchers agree on the positive influence of a school's ethos on teamwork. A culture of teamwork may develop among team members that comprises shared beliefs, values and norms of behaviour about how they work together. It is imperative therefore that the team leader clarifies with the team the positive, constructive behaviours they want the team to do, as opposed to what the team should *not* do.

These expectations, actions, and behaviours form the basis of team performance, first presented by Westerbeek and Smith.

Figure 4.1 Westerbeek and Smith's hierarchy of team needs (2005)

Bringing together a number of researchers' views on the relationship between the school as a team and smaller teams within the school, there are a number of factors that have a positive influence and others that have a negative influence. Being aware of these enables the team leader to manage the team and the situation in which the team is working as effectively as possible.

School-wide cultural norms: factors affecting the team

Positive influences	Negative influences
Clear purpose	Unclear purpose
Consensual decisions	Unilateral decisions
Democratic	Hierarchical
Effectual working	Ineffectual working
Communicative	Uncommunicative
Meaningful communication	Meaningless communication
Informality	Formality
Ability to listen	Inability to listen
Trust	Distrust
Open	Closed
Honest	Dishonest
Embraces conflict	Rejects conflict
Embraces open conflict	Embraces private conflict
Fosters enquiry	Rejects enquiry
Fosters reflection	Rejects reflection
Evaluation of work is norm	Evaluation of work is rare

This table is a powerful checklist for any team leader to return to every couple of months to ensure that they maintain strong team leadership for them and their team.

Top tip ...

Promote a constructive, positive team ethos (team expectations, actions, and behaviours), especially the expectation to support each other.

Team ethos: create alignment within the team

When we are working together as a team we are working *together*. This requires everyone in the team (especially the team leader) to understand the work of the team and everyone's place within that work. When I was preparing a training session for a school and doing the background research for it, I came across some great work in the area of team dynamics by an American researcher and writer, Fred Fiedler. My interpretation of a key point he made around team dynamics is encapsulated here.

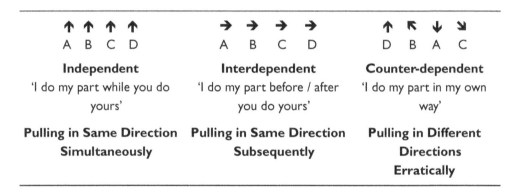

↑ ↑ ↑ ↑	→ → → →	↑ ↖ ↓ ↘
A B C D	A B C D	D B A C
Independent	**Interdependent**	**Counter-dependent**
'I do my part while you do yours'	'I do my part before / after you do yours'	'I do my part in my own way'
Pulling in Same Direction Simultaneously	**Pulling in Same Direction Subsequently**	**Pulling in Different Directions Erratically**

As a team, we successfully work together in two ways; we all get on with our respective jobs, independent of each other towards a collective goal, or we work together interdependently, me completing my part of the work and handing it onto you, with you then completing your part of the work and handing it onto the next person, and so on until the work is complete.

Reflect and apply this to some of the work you are doing. Advertising for and filling a job vacancy is interdependent teamwork, for example. A job description, person specification, and advert need writing/updating before the advert can be sent out before shortlisting can occur and subsequent interviews take place. Teaching lessons, on the other hand, is an independent team activity. The English department team can all teach their lessons independent of both the Maths department and each other. With all teachers able to teach independent of each other, it means the required teaching for that period gets done.

Where things can go awry is when teams in schools and school leaders don't fully understand the process of teamwork as outlined above and do things in their own way, either due to being efficient, or not understanding the process (D in the third column), receiving insufficient/unclear guidance as to what to do or how to do it (B in the third column), just being downright difficult (A in the third column), or possibly being disorganised, rushing the work, and completing it later than it should have been done (C in the third column).

 Top tip ...

When a team is working independently or interdependently, the team is working well. When a team is counter-dependent, a lot of energy is expended in the wrong way and in the wrong direction.

In addition, as can be seen in the figure, when staff are working independently, or interdependently, the team are pulling in the same direction and are easy to manage. When they are not pulling in the same direction (singular), staff are difficult to manage as they are working in different directions (plural) and are thus more difficult to manage. Not only that, as schools work within a fixed timescale, with fixed resources and fixed time frames, any time or energy wastage is ill-affordable. In short, when a team is counter-dependent, a lot of energy is expended in the wrong way and in the wrong direction. As a result, it is important that the team leader frames the team's energy, boxing it in by providing clear direction and clear work parameters, explaining to the team whether the work is independent or interdependent, being clear about:

- The overall process

- What to do and how to do the work

- Key deadlines

 Top tip ...

Frame the team's energy by providing clear direction and clear work parameters.

Team ethos: create team alignment with the school

Every team in a school needs to live and breathe the school's values and ethos. What is your school's motto? How well do your team and their collective work embody this motto? Key qualities at the heart of almost all schools' mottos/ethos is the centrality of learning, the necessity for positivity, ambition, and support, which as a result support a collective identity with pupils being at the centre of everything they do. How does the school's ethos help create team alignment?

Promoting positivity: The school's ethos establishes an expectation for all within the school community to behave, relate, and work constructively and positively, including teaching, collective working, and peer-to-peer support. As such, there are fewer issues for individual teams and the team leader to manage.

Providing support: There is an expectation that the school (and therefore each team within it) support each other, requiring staff to be open to giving support. This may not always be the case, especially when for a particular team, disingenuous or insensitive expectations are in place. Similarly, there is a risk that a school's ethos may require staff to be overly collaborative or excessively supportive, which as a result means there may be insufficient necessary challenge to staff, to students, or to teamwork.

Having a collective identity: The school's ethos provides a collective representation of the school's unique positive values to the (school) community, which means a stronger team identity, a strong standard of expected working practices and a unified front when the school/team present to others. Occasionally, that collective presence of the school's unique positive values may be so strong as to provide overly restrictive/inflexible working practices for teams within the school, such as the need to 'share' the personal and the professional, and not always allow for necessary challenge and accountability.

Top tip ...

Ensure your team's values are in line with the school's ethos and values of the centrality of learning, positivity, ambition, and support.

Having a lived culture of values: The school's ethos, when embedded in culture, makes the school's positive values real and tangible, whereas when they are transient values, they are less embedded and hence less effective. Additionally, where there is a culture of arrogance, or subversion from students, team members, other staff, parents, or governors, it promotes negative behaviour, relationships and a less-friendly atmosphere and means more issues for teams and team leaders to manage.

Prioritising the pupils: All schools should prioritise and promote a 'pupils first' and 'positive pupil outcomes' ethos, which means a positive reputation for the school; however, occasionally, contrary to this, the staff may believe they have a priority over pupils, which requires correction by the team or the team leader.

Having an 'esprit de corps': The expectation that the team do what is expected of them, such as their duties, means the community has a high sense of achievement and can carry on doing their work effectively with a strong sense of 'esprit de corps'. Alternatively, where those expectations are not met creates a negative pressure on others and means the team and the school community do not work as effectively as they could, decreasing that sense of 'esprit de corps'.

4.8 Team expectations: managing the expected and the unexpected

Managing expectations: deliver what is expected, but watch the workload

Almost every school leader has two weaknesses, saying 'yes' when asked to support and wanting to get things done. Indeed, delivery, either through helping others or getting the job done, helps the team feel good in their performance and therefore is a positive influence on the team. However, the additional workload around delivery, and the requirement for the team to perform, is not just as a result of government demands for schools to perform but as a result of having to manage both the expected (that within their control) as well as the unexpected (that which is out of their control).

Managing expectations: not delivering results has a negative effect on the team

Furthermore, the expectation to perform increases pressure and workload on the team, especially when they are not performing and slows school improvement for some, but for others helps drive school improvement. Where expectations are not met, the team/school is judged negatively, meaning a lower reputation, which as a result, especially among parents, has a negative knock-on effect on the school roll.

Managing expectations: set aside time to manage the expected *and* the unexpected

Things that are significant challenges and out of team control means the team/staff do not deliver as much as they could and issues need to be sorted. However, when the team/staff deliver, it can be brilliant. Furthermore, the absence of individuals means teamwork does not get done and can add to the workload of the team, which negatively impacts on their work.

Thus, a key recommendation is for team leaders to set aside time to manage their workload more effectively – for the known and for that which, at the start of the day, is unknown. This will help them prioritise their time and ensure that what needs to be delivered is delivered and continues to have a positive influence on the team.

 Top tip ...

Set aside time each day to manage both the expected (e.g. three things that must be done today) and the unexpected.

4.9 Team expectations: summary

Key ingredient one: clear expectations – clarifying team progress

Influence on the team: helping meet expectations
Impact: increasing team success and reputation

Key takeaways	Key messages
➤ **Set out a clear vision, strategy, and SMART targets** that are achievable, deliverable, and help the team be clear about future actions.	• Have realistically ambitious goals • Have short-term and long-term plans • Ensure your vision and strategy are comprehensive, coherent, and clear • Have SMART rather than unSMART targets • Keep targets clear and simple • Set targets with collective agreement • Working efficiently = setting online targets over a number of years
➤ Ensure you and the team are clear about the **statutory expectations/ requirements** on the team and that these are always evident and secure.	• Frequently review and update all statutory policies and procedures, especially with regard to: o Administration and finance o Admissions o Assessment o Behaviour and attendance o Careers guidance o Curriculum o Early Years Foundation Stage o Governance

Continued on next page

Key takeaways	Key messages
	o Looked-after children
	o Safeguarding
	o SEN
	o Staff employment and teachers pay
➢ Have clear, aligned **roles and responsibilities** in place that minimise overlap, confusion, and create strong personal accountability.	• Have clear job descriptions and an organogram • Maximise team strength through distributed leadership
➢ Have a balanced process of **accountability**, of each other and the team, which celebrates positive progress and strengthens areas of development,	• Holding each other to account is as effective as others doing the same
➢ Engender a strong positive **team ethos** (team expectations, actions, and behaviours) that has a positive influence on teamwork, especially the expectation that team members support each other.	• Ensure the department/school have a clear team ethos • Create alignment within the team • Create team alignment with the school • Provide support • Have a collective identity • Have a lived culture of values • Prioritise the pupils • Have an 'esprit de corps'
➢ Set aside time each day to **manage both the expected** (e.g. three things that must be done today) **and the unexpected**.	• Deliver what is expected, but watch the workload • Not delivering results has a negative effect on the *team* • Set aside time to manage your expected work demands; set aside time to also manage others' unexpected work demands.

5 Key ingredient 2: team interactions – securing team connectivity

Influence on the team: increasing interactions

Impact: increasing team connectivity and effectiveness

5.1 Introduction

This chapter provides clarification as to what we mean by interactions, the influence and impact on the team and others when we get our interactions wrong, but more importantly, when we get our interactions right. It unpacks in more detail the importance of the four Cs – communication, cooperation, collaboration, and consultation with different stakeholders. Communication is explored first, outlining the best ways to communicate within a team and what happens when there is too much communication. This is followed by an exploration of informal and formal communication, the merits of both and when (and when not) to use them. This is followed by a look into the best ways to communicate efficiently as a team and the pros and cons of social media and the internet. When there is communication within a team, there is connectivity; when there is connectivity, there follows a need to support each other when required, creating a sense of camaraderie within the team. One of the key purposes of being in a team is to ensure that the decisions being made within the team are as sound as they can possibly be. Thus, collaboration is explored in further detail. Finally, the ability to consult within the team, but also more widely with others, is a key skill that, if present, can significantly benefit the team and is covered in detail at the end of this chapter. Throughout, the chapter offers top tips and key principles to develop and improve team interaction further.

5.2 Audit: team interactions

To clarify the extent to which your team or school's interactions are in place and working well, consider completing this short audit, either by yourself or with

DOI: 10.4324/9781003303404-5

the rest of the team/school. Once completed, you will be able to identify the interactions that require immediate action (interactions that need to be in place/need urgent revision); interactions that require short-term action (interactions that need tweaking/need to be more consistent) or that require medium-term action, identifying the team's/school's next steps.

Team interactions audit	Positive measure	In place working well	In place needs tweaking	In place needs much work	Not in place	Negative measure
Collaboration	Full collaboration					No collaboration
Consultation	Full consultation					No consultation
Communication (face-to-face)	Sufficient communication					Insufficient communication
Communication (written)	Sufficient communication					Insufficient communication
Within the team	Sufficient communication					Insufficient communication
With students	Sufficient communication					Insufficient communication
With staff	Sufficient communication					Insufficient communication
With parents	Sufficient communication					Insufficient communication
With others	Sufficient communication					Insufficient communication

Follow up:

Immediate action (expectations need to be in place/need urgent revision):

Short-term action (need tweaking/need to be more consistent):

Medium-term action (identify next steps):

My research identified communication as the most important factor to influence the effectiveness of a team and had both positive and negative influences on the work of the team. Here are three core facets to that influence: communication within the team, informal and formal communication, and communication with others outside the team.

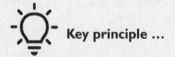

Key principle ...

Communication is the most influential factor on teamwork.

Get it right; watch the team fly. Get it wrong ...

5.3 Internal communication: maintaining healthy communication within the team

Internal team communication: communicate quickly and efficiently within the team

Schools are fast-paced, complex organisations. This means frequent communication is essential to support fast responsive action and quick, effective decision-making. Communication on a frequent basis gives current knowledge to a situation and the ability to re-prioritise urgent/important work. This facilitates a current and shared knowledge to be had by the team, which enables them to show a united front to the school. Using email when not in meetings or teaching, walkie-talkies when out and about, or online concurrent programmes such as Microsoft Teams to share information quickly are all to be recommended.

However, a fast-paced context can also create high pressure, confusion, and stress. Time spent reading and responding to emails is time spent away from doing more important urgent things. Time spent on doing the more urgent important things, means the inbox email number rising into the hundreds, with the subsequent risk to mental wellbeing and the possibility of urgent communications going unread.

Team talk: communication

We all know that communication in a team is key, but you sometimes can have too much of a good thing. I have worked with a number of team leaders who enjoy sending emails and leading through them. For me, this is a passive aggressive way of communicating. Sending a flurry of emails to the team means the team leader lacks visibility with the team, staff, and students as they remain locked in the office and tied to the computer. Similarly, for the team, they have to be on the receiving end, effectively immobilising the team, as they also have to be sat next to their computers reading and responding to those emails rather than being out and about doing other more visible work. What also happens when work is mainly conducted by email, is that more important emails get quickly buried under a mountain of more recent emails. This way of working is also true when using programmes such as Microsoft Teams. Important messages or shared documents in the chat can quickly be buried under more recent chat.

On the other extreme, I have also worked with team leaders who send very few emails. This has the opposite effect, being frustrating for the team, as it is difficult to know what is going on and leaves a sense within the team of factionalism ('other people know what's going on…') and frustration ('… and I don't').

What works well is to summarise the team's week's work in one email. This reduces the number of emails that need to be sent (therefore being efficient, clarifies for the team

Continued on next page

what their part is in the work needing to be done, is good for cumulative knowledge and cross-checks you have not forgotten anything, and keeps everyone in the picture). Or, if preferred, a short 5-minute briefing each morning to notice issues from the previous day and ensure all is set fair for the present day keeps communication efficient and meaningful.

Whichever way the team wishes to communicate, agreeing team communication protocols is the key.

Top tip ...

Communicate sufficiently with the team. This supports and strengthens the team's cumulative knowledge. However, too much communication can impede action not support it. Be aware!

For all team members, especially leaders, it is important to learn the skills of skim reading and touch typing, especially reading and responding to communications from those higher up the line management tree. This will ensure you are, and are seen to be, as on top of the situation as you can be.

In addition, I am sure you have sat in meetings where people talk for far longer than is needed, or expected, if there is a timed agenda. Similarly, I am sure you have been sent unnecessarily long emails that simply waste everyone's time when having to wade through them. Having clear parameters in place (see Chapter 7 – infrastructure) to ensure these things do not happen is key to efficient and effective internal team communication.

Top tip ...

Learn the skills of skim reading and touch typing, especially reading and responding to communications from those higher up.

Internal team communication: connect together with professionalism, respect, and humour

At work, the first bond between a team is that they have all been brought together for their ability to do the job. Thus, we sometimes forget that our first, fundamental relationship with each other as staff in a team in schools is as professionals. In addition, everyone will have had an interview of some description, with checks completed and satisfactory references sought. As such, each member of staff has been chosen above others. Therefore, all staff must treat each other at all times as professionals and with due respect because they were the best person for the job at the time and come to work for the same reasons as everybody else. When this is not the case, it should be followed up in accordance with the school's policies and procedures. From the research I carried out with six teams from across the country, working with respect and professionalism had a positive influence on the team and a negative influence when the team were disrespectful and unprofessional with each other. No surprises there, but it still happens and so team leaders still therefore need to manage these things accordingly.

In addition, humour was also a key part of informal internal communication that enabled relationships to develop, with work pressures and tensions able to be released in a healthy way. As such, humour helps facilitate the team having fun together, the team venting and showing a human side to their work.

Top tip ...

Always connect with each other as professionals, with respect and humour.

5.4 Communication: utilise informal and formal communication wisely

From the first 'Morning!' to the last 'Have a good evening!', we are in almost constant communication throughout the day. Whether, teaching, leading, or supporting both, in schools, communication is the currency of our work. For school leaders, it is important to understand the difference between informal and formal communication and how to use these well. It is important to understand the difference between informal and formal communication and how to use these well.

At a basic level, formal communication can be considered as anything that is written and shared with others at work, for example, emails, meeting minutes, letters, policies, documents. Informal communication can be considered as anything that is said, a conversation, a chat, etc., when not at work.

Therefore, for the record, anything said at work is on the record. Why? Because you are *at work*. However, there are some occasions at work where it is necessary to speak 'off the record'. How do you as a leader approach this? Whenever you need to speak off the record, it is important to preface what you are about to say with 'taking my leadership hat off for a moment', which enables you and the other person to speak as people rather than professionals. It also helps keep the situation clear by saying at the end, 'Right, leadership hat is now back on'.

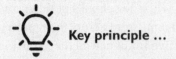

Key principle ...

All communication at work is on the record.

Setting up a WhatsApp group or Teams group enables the team to communicate informally outside of school hours and may work well. Within my research, the team's ability to use informal and formal communication effectively helped share understanding and knowledge and facilitated good decision-making and vice versa. Indeed, clear, direct communication, especially in meetings, meant greater synergy and more effective work and vice versa, with online and internal communication methods viewed as being clearer and more efficient. Where communication was unclear, or ineffective, wasted both time and money and meant the team was unable to effectively perform its responsibilities.

Team talk: Nipping issues in the bud informally before having to address them formally

One of the issues as a new headteacher or new Head of Department is inheriting a team that do not get on. I remember taking over a team and when I asked a colleague to liaise with another member of the team, their response was 'I don't speak to her, we don't get on'. My response was 'I'm not asking you to get on with them, simply to liaise with them. Please sort out the issues you have between yourselves informally first before I have to step in and sort things out formally.'

It is natural from time to time that communication does not go as well as it should. A well-meant apology can do much to heal an upset or build a bridge. Similarly, understanding that most grievance and complaints policies require staff to sort things out wherever possible, informally first, requires staff to do exactly that – sort things out informally first. When this is unsuccessful, that is when the Head of Department or the headteacher has to step in.

Top tip ...

Understand the difference between informal and formal communication, official and unofficial communication, and how to manage these.

5.5 Team communication: utilise digital media to communicate efficiently

Mode of communication	Advantages	Disadvantages
Conference calls	• Connect anywhere • Efficient communication with multiple recipients at once • Quick collaboration • Quick decision-making	• Dependence on group availability • Inability to record views for future reference
Online group communications, e.g. Microsoft Teams, WhatsApp, or Zoom	• Connect anywhere • Efficient communication with multiple recipients at once • Quick collaboration • Quick decision-making	• Dependence on group availability
Emails	• Connect anywhere • Efficient communication with multiple recipients at once • Potential for quick collaboration • Potential for quick decision-making • Records views for future reference	• Once sent, gets buried underneath later emails • Inability to communicate concurrently • Necessity of waiting for others to respond before moving things forward
Online platforms for: Concurrent editing, e.g. Google Docs Shared areas, e.g. DropBox/Moodle Evaluation, e.g. Mentimeter or Survey Monkey	• Connect anywhere • Efficient communication with multiple recipients at once • Potential for quick decision making • Quick collaboration • Records views for future reference	• Left unmanaged, grow into an online storeroom of old obsolete documents • Can be large, cumbersome, and inefficient when searching for key documents

As can be seen from the table above, conference calls and online communication today enable the team to connect with each other anywhere, to efficiently communicate with multiple recipients at once, facilitates quick collaboration, and, as a result, quick decision-making. The main difference between the advantages of these ways of communicating is in the ability to record the communication for future reference, i.e. conference calls and Zoom meetings, by their nature of being predominantly oral, require an additional mechanism to record proceedings, whereas other modes of communication, being written, inherently are recorded for future reference.

Each, though, has its unique disadvantages. The immediate communications of conference calls, Zoom meetings, or Team conversations require the whole team to be present. Their absence during the meeting, call, or conversation means a break in the chain of communication, with potentially diminished communication, collaboration, and decision-making as a result.

Emails, while being the mode of communication without equal, are particularly troublesome. An email sent at 9 a.m. will be top of the inbox and most likely to be read and responded to. By 3 p.m., it is likely to have been buried underneath 40 or 50 other emails with the likelihood of receiving no response, especially a response needed urgently. This compounds team ineffectiveness if team members are waiting for a response before they can move onto the next stage of their work, i.e. if the teamwork is interdependent, another mode of communication other than email, is preferable.

 Top tip ...

If the teamwork is interdependent, another mode of communication other than email is preferable.

Emails were viewed as demanding and meant increased workload for the team, even though they created an opportunity to confer and share good practice. Similarly, inappropriate or demanding emails meant a higher priority was given to them and created stress, although receiving positive emails meant a higher morale and positive wellbeing.

A large issue for schools with emails is the timing of them being sent and received. It should not be the case that because I choose to send an email at 9.00 p.m. at night because that suits my lifestyle, it should be read and responded to by the rest of the team at 9.01 p.m. Using technology smartly, delaying the sending of non-urgent emails to hours that are during the school day, is the preferable way to support team well-being.

Top tip ...

To communicate efficiently and effectively: understand the pros and cons of teamwork through social media and the internet.

5.6 Team co-operation (internal): united we stand and are stronger

Team presence is key

The one significant factor to influence team effectiveness is team presence. In other words, if the team are not here, other people will have to do their work, potentially doubling the work of others at no extra pay or having to pay someone to do the work in their absence, doubling the cost.

Having to cover for other staff means the team are not able do their own work. In my research, a participant team leader encapsulated it succinctly, 'when you've got a member of the team who would be dealing with a lot of that, we don't have that buffer, it comes straight to me or another member of the team' taking up time to chase things up, which was frustrating. The presence of team members and them doing their job, meant the team could get on and do their work, which saved time for the team. Thus, having a clear understanding of the daily work for yourself and the team that *must* be done and work that *could* be done is important in safeguarding our own and the team's essential work.

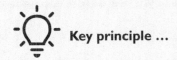

Key principle ...

Team absence either doubles the work for the team or doubles the cost to the team

Team talk: share the burden; share the success

Working together on key documents or contributing your part to the collective whole helps the team work efficiently. A good example of this was as Head of Performing Arts I created a student-friendly assessment grid of the key skills in Music: practising, rehearsing, performing, composing, and improvising. Liaising with the rest of the team,

Continued on next page

they could see how, with a few small tweaks, such a set of descriptors could be used, especially in Dance and Drama, and to some extent in Art and PE. We therefore created a similar set of descriptors, displayed in a similar way in all the classrooms. This ensured we had consistent discussions and consistent formative assessment procedures across the department. When Ofsted and two teacher training universities came to visit, they were impressed and took them away to share as evidence of best practice. This gave a real boost to the team in being able to gain external validation for the team's success in an area that was common to each of us.

 Top tip ...

Have a clear understanding of your and the team's daily work that *must* be done and work that *could* be done, so that our own and the team's essential daily work is successfully completed.

5.7 Co-operation (external): ensure your work is externally validated

Working with key external agencies such as the Department for Education (DfE), Ofsted, unions, and Local Education Authorities (LEAs) to ensure our work is compliant and current is important for any team in a school. However, this can bring additional pressure to the team if not managed carefully. Below, I outline how a team leader can ensure working with external agencies is as appositive an experience as possible.

Co-operation: government

Government demands: The constantly changing work demanded by government of schools means different work, wasted work, and disrupted routines for staff and students in schools, and in my research was the main cause of additional wasted workload. Furthermore, unclear government demands require extra time and create additional workload, diminishing staff and team morale if not managed carefully, but occasionally, helpful, clear demands can improve team time and workload. Indeed, when the work demanded by the DfE matches the direction of school improvement, although creating more work, school routines will improve.

In a similar way, a lack of government consultation can mean poor communication and undermines team confidence in the team leader but can also create an opportunity to communicate more with stakeholders than is usual.

On the negative side, changing or multiple government targets can mean unachievable or unachieved targets for the team and hence more challenging work for the team. Moreover, with team targets being directed or influenced by unfair, or politically motivated, government criteria can mean having to complete work that is irrelevant and constraining. In addition, urgent government directives that demand immediate action mean other (important) work has to be put to one side.

As government strategy is more likely to be short term and populist rather than long term and coherent, this seeming lack of a long-term strategy from the government can undermine confidence and coherence in the work of the team.

 Top tip ...

Protect your team from excessive governmental demands. Do what is statutorily required; other work can be left to the team's discretion.

Co-operation: Department for Education

The findings of my research are consistent with the findings of other researchers in relation to the Department for Education (DfE) in that it is a combination of both a positive influence through its inspection arm, Ofsted (securing improved results for the students), and a negative influence (creating new demands, increasing workload) on teamwork. This has been no truer than the last two years, during a pandemic. The pressure on schools to manage the incessant and constantly changing demands of the DfE has been intense. This, coupled with the lack of consultation and the lack of funding experienced by all schools, adds to the negative influence of the DfE on schools during a pandemic.

In addition, with two references to 'teams' in the Standards of Excellence for team leaders, five references in the revised National Professional Qualifications for Senior Leaders framework, and no specific reference to teams in the ten requirements in both documents, continues a cultural blindness to the importance of teamwork at team level in schools by the DfE. In this, the findings of my research concur with other researchers in that there is minimal Continuing Professional Development (CPD) for teams, especially government-supported CPD, and due to the importance of their work as a team, more consideration and support should be given to teamwork in that CPD.

Co-operation: Ofsted

There appears to be little research on the influence of inspections on leadership in schools. What little there is, on staff wellbeing, either does not review the impact of inspections on staff wellbeing or suggests it is unsupportive. As such, my research on the influence of inspections on teamwork highlighted the positive confirmation of inspections of teamwork, as well as the more negative influence of inspection judgements being regarded as unfair. In other words, on the one hand, Ofsted provide the school with reassurance and, on the other, the mixed blessing of the Ofsted judgement.

Indeed, inspections administers external accountability, which reinforces and validates best practice, sharpens school practice, and makes you know your stuff, so you are on point, providing reassurance that you and your team are compliant. However, participants in the research noted that when different inspections are inspecting the same thing, it can be a waste of time (two responses) and add to workload.

In contrast, although inspections can be supportive and helpful and positive/fair judgements mean lots of praise for good work done, they can highlight areas that the team need to (re)consider, which then evoke conflicting responses. Moreover, inspection judgements can be brutal, and, as such, responded to disproportionately, providing biased or conflicting judgements that are unhelpful and mean unfair judgements are made of the school and the team by stakeholders.

 Top tip ...

For any team (and therefore any team leader), this is the badge without equal. Have a clear plan of action that is demonstrably secured each term.

Co-operation: competition

Regarding how schools manage the competition with other schools, the pressure for schools to beat their competition means a high pressure on teams in the school to deliver and creates more worry for them, a need to change their (curriculum) offer and way of working, and therefore more change and more work for the team, especially when competitor schools have the advantage. However, competition forces teams to think creatively and to further develop school strengths to beat the competition.

Top tip ...

Use your competition's strengths and successes as a driver to develop your own team's strengths and attain their own successes. Remember the Olympics: faster, higher, stronger!

Co-operation: industry

Co-operating with local, national, and international businesses can create opportunities for improvement and positive change in schools. The requirements of industry create opportunities for schools to revise and update their ethos and routines so that their work is as good as it can be and cutting edge. However, where these changes in school routines can sometimes be perceived as being driven by industry and not the school or are different to what staff are able to deliver, this can create tension with the staff.

Top tip ...

Co-operate with external colleagues, gaining the external validation that what you do is (working towards) best practice.

5.8 Collaboration: stronger together

In my research, collaboration with others was seen as a positive influence, especially when it was developed between teams and between schools. However, while the schools in my research found the internal collaboration a wholly positive experience, the influence of other schools/education providers externally was both positive (Multi-Academy Trusts) and negative (Local Education Authorities, competitor schools). Internal collaboration can be a positive experience for the team because collectively agreed targets between the team, or between leaders can mean a greater sense of ownership of those targets. From a positive perspective within my research, the overriding and singular view of participants was that collaboration helped contributions to improve, and hence the work of the team improved.

Top tip …

Collaborate with other leaders outside the team or the school and see connections and meaning strengthen as a result.

5.9 Consult with stakeholders: ensure the best decisions are made for the school

Consultation helps facilitate expert input to schoolwork and increases the confidence of leaders to improve the quality of teamwork and schoolwork. Indeed, regarding the influence of stakeholders (students/staff/parents/middle leaders) on teamwork in my research, much of the literature reports on team engagement with, or impact on, these groups. It does not fully discuss how the team may be influenced by these stakeholders. Below is a brief discussion about how stakeholders can influence the interactions and therefore the teamwork in schools.

Consultation is a method by which the team ensures the best decisions are made and everyone is on board. Consultation helps improve staff relationships, the quality and ease of the team's work, and provides valuable feedback, helping get staff on board with team initiatives. However, if there is poor handling of the consultation process, usually by the team leader, this then does not result in the anticipated change and means more challenging work for the team to do, with time taken up proportionately over petty issues when handling these appropriately with staff.

Consultation: students

Student responsiveness: Where students are able to work with staff teams, a positive difference can be made to young people's lives, whereas when students are unable to work with staff teams, less of a difference can be made to young people's lives.

Student maturity/ability: Students' intelligence, maturity and openness can be a pleasure to work with, while students' worry/concerns in response to innovation and personal or institutional change can mean the team needs to respond sensitively. This also shapes how the team lead the school in response to student need, enabling teamwork to be more effective. However, lower student ability or behaviour can mean a lower reputation of the school and more work for the team in managing, occasionally, unrealistic expectations. This can be most noticeable when the achievement of students is a reality and makes it easier to get people on board, with the opposite also being the case.

Student trust: When students do not trust the team, students can be challenging and need dealing with, which can mean lower staff wellbeing/increased frustration on behalf of the team. When students trust staff, they are a pleasure to work with and are a positive influence on staff/team wellbeing.

Demanding students: Demanding students can mean they need dealing with urgently, taking up team time, with the variety of needs requiring a higher prioritisation over other work.

Top tip ...

Collaborate with students, developing their trust and maturity of response, while at the same time reducing the demandingness of students with their issues.

Consultation: staff

Long-term staff: Staff staying for a long time with the school can be seen as beneficial to others in school but can also be expensive, limiting finances being spent elsewhere in school.

Staff buy-in: Talented and helpful staff can mean teamwork is completed more effectively and efficiently, endeavouring to empower staff. However, (unfair) staff misconceptions or assumptions can require additional teamwork/grounding.

Staff mindset: Staff who are professional and driven need less team attention in being supportive, helping manage and deal with issues and saving team time/work, including those who are open to the new, happy to hit the ground running, and go the extra mile. However, staff who are demanding/difficult can cause issues that need attention, requiring a higher prioritisation over other work, creating frustration when the team leader is unable to deal with these, taking up time and slowing school improvement, including those not as open to the new.

Staff absence: Staff absence can also mean variable staff quality when covering colleagues, creating additional work to replace/cover colleagues and can be a drain on finances/creating additional workload for the team, whereas the ability to have staff present/additional staff can increase stability and thus reduce the workload on the team.

Staff communication: Unhelpful staff communication and feedback is draining on the team, whereas helpful communication and feedback can inform better decisions and, as a result, energise teamwork.

Staff high expectations: The staff's high/unrealistic expectations can usually be unmet and can therefore mean challenges from staff; however, the high expectations of talented staff means a high level of performance from their team and their students.

Top tip ...

Collaborate with staff and minimise absence, improve communication, open their mindset, and harness their high expectations.

Consultation: parents and the local community

Parent engagement: A lack of parent involvement/engagement with the school can mean difficulties for a team in engaging parents and can mean a reduction in the school roll, leading to reduced finances. The opposite of this, of course, may also be true. For example, parents who are more engaged and take more responsibility for their children's learning/behaviour can mean fewer difficulties for the team, a stable cohort, and stable finances for the school.

Parent behaviour: Parents can be inappropriate, or very/too challenging in their behaviour, taking up team time and energy in dealing with them, and this can be demotivating for the team. However, some parents are supportive and 'onside', which can increases the team's motivation to work with them.

Parent expectations: Parents with unrealistically high expectations can create significant challenges for the team; however, parents with realistically high expectations support significant aspirations for the team.

Top tip ...

Collaborate with parents, minimise their poor behaviour, maximise their engagement, and harness their high expectations.

Local community

Community liaison: Liaising with the local community builds relationships and brings them into school, enabling a closer communication/relationship with them.

However, it also takes staff away from the school and thus affects their team-work at school, adding time and workload to the team. For example, community expectations that a school can solve all their problems, which in reality, the school cannot. In addition, when there is inappropriate communication from the community, it means that more time and effort is being expended by the team to address these issues.

Community perception: When the local community has a high esteem for the school/team, relationships are good; however, where there is a negative perception/(unfair) prejudice about the work of the team, the reputation of the team is worse than it should be.

Community expectations: When the local community has realistic expectations of the school to solve issues, there is usually less work for the team. However, when these are unrealistic expectations to solve issues in the community, it can mean additional work for the team and being outside of team control meaning prioritising that work over other schoolwork.

 Top tip ...

Collaborate with the local community and create meaningful liaison, improve the community perception of the school, and harness their high expectations.

Governors: governor challenge and support

The challenge and support from governors can mean that the work of the team is more likely to be more considered in the best interests of the school, more manageable and more effective as a result. However, occasionally, the work demanded by governors can be unnecessary to the school's work and create additional work for the team. In addition, where governors are not in alignment with the team, it can make working with the governors harder and vice versa.

Governors: governor hierarchy

The higher status of governors 'above the leadership' can mean their directives need to be followed and need to be prioritised, (usually) above other work.

5.10 Team interactions; summary

Key ingredient two: interactions – securing team connectivity

Influence on the team: increasing interactions
Impact: increasing team connectivity and effectiveness

Key takeaways	Key messages
Internal communication: maintain healthy communication within the team. This supports and strengthens the team's cumulative knowledge. However, too much communication can impede action through too much talk or by creating email slaves. Be (a)ware!	• Maintain healthy communication within the team. • Communicate quickly and efficiently within the team. • Learn the skills of skim reading and touch typing, especially reading and responding to communications from those higher up. • Connect together with professionalism, respect, and humour.
Understand the difference between informal and formal communication, official and unofficial communication, and how to manage these.	• Utilise informal and formal communication wisely. • All communication at work is on the record. • Understand the difference between informal and formal communication, official and unofficial communication, and how to manage these.
Communicate efficiently. Understand the pros and cons of teamwork through social media and the internet.	• Utilise social media and the internet to communicate efficiently. • If the teamwork is interdependent, another mode of communication other than email, is preferable. • To communicate efficiently and effectively, understand the pros and cons of teamwork through social media and the internet.
Co-operate with each other and provide support for colleagues when needed.	• Team presence is key. • Team absence either doubles the work for the team or doubles the cost to the team. • Have a clear understanding of your and the team's daily work that *must* be done and work that *could* be done, so that our own and the team's essential daily work is successfully completed.
Collaborate with other leaders and see connections and meaning strengthen as a result.	• Holding each other to account is as effective as others' doing the same.

Continued on next page

Key takeaways	Key messages
Consult with stakeholders: enjoy the benefits and manage the challenges of working with: o Government and Ofsted o Students o Staff o Parents o Governors	• Protect your team from excessive governmental demands. Do what is statutorily required – other work can be left to the team's discretion. • For any team (and therefore any team leader), this is the badge without equal. Have a clear plan of action that is demonstrably secured each term. • Use your competition's strengths and successes as a driver to develop your own team's strengths and attain their own successes. Remember the Olympics: faster, higher, stronger! • Co-operate with external colleagues, gaining the external validation that what you do is (working towards) best practice. • Collaborate with students, developing their trust and maturity of response, while at the same time reducing the demandingness of students with their issues. • Collaborate with staff and minimise absence, improve communication, open their mindset, and harness their high expectations. • Collaborate with parents, minimise their poor behaviour, maximise their engagement and harness their high expectations. • Collaborate with the local community and create meaningful liaison, improve the community perception of the school, and harness their high expectations.
Consult with colleagues in and out of school so that you have the external validation to show that what you do is best practice.	• Deliver what is expected, but watch the workload. • Not delivering results has a negative effect on the *team*. • Set aside time to manage your expected work demands; set aside time to also manage others' unexpected work demands.

6 Key ingredient 3: team behaviours – building team relationships

Influence on the team: increasing helpful behaviours

Impact: increasing positive team relationships

6.1 Introduction

This chapter provides clarification as to what we mean by team behaviours, the influence and impact on the team and others when we get our team behaviours right and when we get them wrong. It unpacks in more detail the importance of qualities such as openness, loyalty, trust, support, respect, and professionalism. It offers a checklist to help audit a team in relation to their team behaviours and offers case studies and strategies to develop and improve this further.

6.2 Audit: team behaviours

To clarify the extent to which your team or school's behaviours are in place and working well, consider completing this short audit, either by yourself or with the rest of the team/school. Once completed, you will be able to identify the team behaviours that require immediate action (behaviours that need to be in place/need urgent revision), behaviours that require short-term action (behaviours that need tweaking/need to be more consistent), or which require medium-term action, identifying the team's/school's next steps. The following behaviours are not exhaustive. Tweak or change as needed!

 DOI: 10.4324/9781003303404-6

Team behaviours audit	Positive measure	In place working well	In place needs tweaking	In place needs much work	Not in place	Negative measure
Friendliness	Friendly					Unfriendly
Honesty	Honest					Dishonest
Interest	Caring					Uncaring
Loyalty	Loyal					Disloyal/ Subversive
Openness	Open					Closed
Professionalism	Professional					Unprofessional
Respect	Respectful					Disrespectful
Support	Supportive					Unsupportive
Trust	Trustworthy					Untrustworthy

Follow up:

Immediate action (expectations need to be in place/need urgent revision):

Short-term action (need tweaking/need to be more consistent):

Medium-term action (identify next steps):

6.3 Team behaviours: expectations, actions, and behaviours

When looking at team behaviours, whether with a family unit, or in a professional capacity, the starting point for everyone is that their behaviour is normal. This makes sense as they will have known no different either when growing up or beginning work as a professional. They will have been expected to follow their parents' expected line of behaviour since being a child in the case of the family or follow the lead of the Head of Department since starting work, in the case of the professional team.

A personal, slightly embarrassing example of this was when I was a teenager. Saturday night in our household was always bath night ahead of Church on Sunday morning. Little occurred in between. This continued until I was about 14 when friends kept commenting on my hair and how greasy it was. My behaviour was challenged and understanding broadened in that having a bath once a week was not the done thing in every household – a shower or bath a little more frequently was far more the accepted norm in most social circles. In raising the expectation I had of myself, my actions subsequently changed, and as this was occurring every day, my behaviour changed as a result. To improve the effectiveness of the team, identify behaviours that are ineffective, specify actions that need to improve, and raise the expectations that have been set. Thus, expectations lead to actions that when repeated, lead to behaviours:

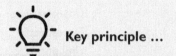

This is the fundamental principle that underpins this chapter, that all behaviour is founded on a set of expectations that may or may not be the best, but that when challenged can lead to improved actions that as a result to increasingly effective teamwork. This leads us nicely to unpacking the five fundamental expectations of a team.

Key principle ...

Expectations clarify actions; repeated actions become behaviours; behaviours produce effective or ineffective working.

Team talk: raising expectations – improving individual action and collective behaviour

A recurring professional example is in the area of school expectations and what this looks like for students, teachers, and leaders. Below is an example of a set of expectations (e.g. be punctual), what this means for individual action for students (be in tutor time at 8.30 a.m.), teachers (be on time greeting students at the classroom door), and leaders (ensure all meetings and lessons start and finish on time).

Expectations of Pupils	Expectations of Staff
Punctual: Be on time	Punctual: Be on time
Routines: Stick to routines	Routines: Insist on routines
Expectations: Follow instructions first time	Expectations: Make expectations clear
Phones: Are on site, Out of sight & Off	Planning: Deliver well-planned lessons
Attitude: Be Calm, Kind, Polite, Honest and Respectful	Attitude: Be Calm, Kind, Polite, Honest and Respectful
Respect: Respect our community and environment	Ready: Have classroom & resources ready for all learners
Equipped: Be fully equipped	Engaging: Have high expectations of learning
Dress: Wear correct uniform	Dress: Wear professional attire

Figure 6.1 Student/staff expectations

6.4 Team behaviours: support

When I studied team norms as part of my doctoral research, five key fundamentals to any teamwork became clear: support, honesty, openness, respect, and trust. Of course, it is possible to name a number of expectations different to these five, but almost all researchers I read incorporated these five as intrinsic to teamwork.

With support, there is connectivity, there is me looking out for you and vice versa. Support is the 'we' before 'me'. Without support, we are an island and not a team. With honesty in any relationship, the foundation is solid; it may be a little uncomfortable at times (even very uncomfortable!), but everyone knows where they stand. With dishonesty, as the parable in the Bible suggests, it is a house built on sand, on shifting illusion and untruths. No teamwork can survive deception. Similarly, a team that is open, open to new ideas, new people, new ways of working protects itself from becoming fossilised and obsolete. In a similar way to honesty, mutual respect and trust is the glue between people that truly makes a team. Each one of these areas is covered in a little more detail below, but suffice to say, without the basics being in place for any team of support, honesty, openness, respect, and trust, the team will go nowhere. Expect support, honesty, openness, respect, and trust from every team member as they are the key foundation stones to effective teamwork.

 Top tip ...

Without the basics being in place of support, honesty, openness, respect, and trust, the team will go nowhere.

Support: expect the team to be there for each other, putting the 'we' before 'me'

Support is a key foundation stone to effective teamwork. Being there for each other, putting the 'we' before 'me' to further develop the cohesion and sense of 'togetherness' within the team, is key to the effectiveness of the team. Working with others and other team members in a supportive way is an effective way of working, as being supportive of the staff within the school is a strength to be developed, because the presence of internal or external support enables teamwork to grow and be stronger, and the absence of internal or external support, means teamwork does not grow and is not stronger. Similarly, being on hand can provide personalised support and means issues are dealt with more effectively but can take up time. In addition, though supporting others must usually be prioritised over other work, it ultimately benefits the team. Within the school, team support can manifest itself in a number of ways: through the team or school's ethos, the need for collective acceptance, for unity, and to help the team guard against peer pressure.

Team talk: supporting each other – duties

A significant example of team support that came out of both my research and professional experience is that of teammates doing their duties. Doing a duty (being on the corridor at break time or in the playground at lunchtime) is key in that it provides the important statutory safeguarding requirements schools need to have in place while students (and staff) are having a break. Not doing a duty, due to meetings being scheduled during a duty, or meetings, lessons, or assemblies overrunning, leaves space for issues to occur and the school failing to provide the level of safeguarding that is needed. It is frequently the niggle with other team members that creates most dissent or provides the most visible support. Either way, it is an important and easily fixable thing to get right and for the team to demonstrate its support for each other.

Team ethos: support is a given

The collective representation of the school or team's vision and values through the team's collectively unified behaviour embeds the concept of team support in everyday team behaviour, for example, everyone being on duty or working together constructively on a key project. When the team actively supports each other, work is shared; however, this means that when supporting others, this could create additional work for yourself.

Collective acceptance: we support everyone in the team, whatever their foibles

The team is more cohesive and supportive of each other when everybody in the team accepts that they are stronger together and vice versa. A key point here is in being able to accept each other's strengths and weaknesses and being non-accusatory when working together. This can mean greater team cohesion and enable a greater sharing of work and shared understanding to exist between the team, raising their collective awareness to maximise team strength and minimise team weakness. Especially when the team are solutions-focused, this benefits team and staff relationships. Like a Swiss Army knife, when the team are solutions-focused it means the situation improves/more problems are solved; however, not being solutions-focused means staff can be more dogmatic and unprepared to compromise.

 Top tip ...

As a team be pragmatic. Like a Swiss Army knife, the team uses its diverse skills, knowledge, and qualities to successfully tackle any issue.

Unity: praise in public; criticise in private

A mutual appreciation supports a sense of team togetherness and helps present a united front to the rest of the school; however, a lack of mutual appreciation supports a lack of sense of team togetherness and does not help the team present a united front.

Peer pressure: do not let the side down

The team is stronger and more cohesive when each team member is not influenced by pressure from others outside the team. Furthermore, peer pressure holds the team together but can also be a negative pressure on team members to 'not let the side down'. For example, when team members carry out their duties, the rest of the school community can carry on with their work. However, the team expectation to be 'available all the time' means prioritising duties over other work, thus demanding more time. Moreover, dealing with issues from duties can take up precious time and add more to the team's workload.

Team loyalty: above all else, be loyal

One of the strongest behaviours team members can exhibit in supporting their team is in being loyal to that team. In my research, it came out as a very strong influence on the team, both positively and negatively. Therefore it is important for team leaders to develop loyalty in their team; if not, disloyalty can expose weaknesses within the team and allows staff to capitalise on those. This is especially true when team members put their own interests over those of the team and they become disloyal, their loyalty being placed in individual self-interest rather than in the interests of the team.

6.5 Team behaviours: honesty

Honesty is a key foundation stone to effective teamwork. Being honest, which includes not lying as well as not being economical with the truth, is key to strong communication and shows that the team has integrity and a degree of incorruptibility. If you are dishonest with a team member, you are ultimately being dishonest to the team. Just like in a family, if you bruise one family member, you bruise them all.

The presence of honesty in teamwork helps promote professionalism and the collective understanding of the team. For example, those that are able to say exactly how they are feeling and then have that out in a professional way, are more conducive to teamwork than when staff are not as honest with people as they could be. Conversely, where staff are dishonest with each other it means being unable or choosing to not manage the personal over the professional.

 Top tip ...

Honesty really is the best policy. Being honest with each other gets to the heart of any issue (and therefore any solution) quickly.

6.6 Team behaviours: openness

Openness is a key foundation stone to effective teamwork. Being open is not just about being transparent in what we do (which could be interpreted as being honest) but is also about being open to new ideas, open to criticism, open to reflection. Openness is the opposite to being closed or fixed, most eloquently portrayed by Carol Dweck in her seminal work *Mindset*, promoting the view from her research that successful people (and by implication, successful teams) have an 'open' rather than a 'fixed' mindset.

Being open and honest with each other as a team means that issues can get sorted within the team and helps promote unity within the team and rightly portrays a sense of unity outside the team. However, when team members are not open to team colleagues, showing a modicum of dishonesty and disloyalty, can mean getting issues sorted outside the team, exposing issues within the team, and fundamentally not helping the team move forward. Being open with each other also develops the leadership of the team and others, helping the team make better decisions, develops the potential in others, and enables innovative ideas for team/school improvement to emerge. In addition, open communication means staff or pupils, or parents, are less likely to be dissenting, and more likely to be on board with the team and can mean fewer issues and less workload for them team, facilitating a recognition being given to those that deserve it and is something everyone can value.

However, there can be a risk that being too open, especially to new ideas and initiatives, can detract from the core work of the school (providing and outstanding education to the pupils). Especially for the team leader, it is important not to say 'Yes' to everything!

Top tip ...

Be open to new ideas and initiatives but be careful not to say 'yes' to everything.

Team talk: know thyself (being open with each other) – the Johari window

A useful and empowering activity to help have a clearer understanding of the team is to complete what is known as a Johari window with each other. This is where a list of approximately 25 adjectives are ticked as to which apply to each member of the team. Each team member also completes one for themselves. When the adjectives are combined, it enables the team to be clearer about the:

Individual adjectives **present** in the team (adjectives ticked by both the individual and others)

Collective adjectives **present** in the team (adjectives ticked by more than one individual and others)

Individual adjectives to be **questioned** in the team (adjectives ticked by the individual but not others)

Collective adjectives to be **questioned** in the team (adjectives ticked by more than one individual but not others)

Individual adjectives to be **promoted** in the team (adjectives not ticked by the individual but ticked by others)

Collective adjectives to be **promoted** in the team (adjectives not ticked by more than one individual but ticked by others)

Individual adjectives **not present** in the team (adjectives not ticked by both the individual and others)

Collective adjectives **not present** in the team (adjectives not ticked by more than one individual and others)

6.7 Team behaviours: respect and professionalism

Respect is a key foundation stone to effective teamwork. It is critical to effective teamwork that you show professional respect for each other at all times (we are, after all, being paid to do a job). Effectively managing any personal disrespect you may have constructively (diplomatically ignore or tactfully, constructively feedback) is key.

In my research, like safety, respect occurred in the literature as part of Maslow's influential Hierarchy of Needs and is a necessity, or pre-condition, to effective teamwork taking place. My research asserts that respect should be considered as a norm within the team and thus help develop team confidence.

Team leaders play an integral part in modelling the team, setting the team's priorities, and supporting the team to behave professionally as a team. This improves staff wellbeing, especially in supporting members of the team to more effectively manage the personal over the professional. Ensuring there is professional respect at all times within and from the team, helps reduce significant issues, which would otherwise take important time and energy away from supporting and improving teaching and learning.

As a participant in the research observed of their team meetings:

> We've got a very cosmopolitan set of personalities within the team, ranging from the highly energetic and articulate and driving and ambitious, to the really quite belligerent and 'I'm not moving, because I'm right', and really everything in between that. So, what that has meant is that very often getting the agenda items through is as much about winning the personalities on the team, as well as actually getting through the agenda items.

Be respectful and professional at all times. Behaving professionally can mean the team are more organised and effective as a team and more efficient with their time. Furthermore, being professional enables the team to destress in a safe environment.

 Top tip ...

Manage team issues quickly, and nip them in the bud. As much as possible, the team's time and energy should be focused on delivering high-quality teaching and learning – nothing else.

Subversion: be ruthless in challenging both active and passive team subversion

Subversion is a cancer to teamwork and needs dealing with swiftly if it is not to take hold and completely kill any effective teamwork. Subversion can be actively or passively carried out, usually by team members with an unresolved gripe from the past.

All schools in my research indicated that they had to deal with subversive staff within and outside their teams. This tended to be linked to a lack of effective accountability as all schools indicated that the staff also had a tendency (usually historically) to 'get away with it'. This was in line with the literature, which suggested that subversive team players can undermine the effective working of the team, through being uncooperative, uncollaborative, and distrustful. Team leaders in the research did not feel able to deal effectively with either the active or passive subversion beyond making sure they were on board, which led back to the quality of documentation, such as job descriptions and policies being in place, rigorous, and up to date. It is thus important for the team to have clear, up-to-date documentation in place, including accountability measures, to minimise the negative influence of subversion on the team.

Active subversion was when individuals or groups actively worked to undermine and challenge the work of the team, and meant difficult working relationships occurred and slowed down team progress, with subversive comments or actions needing to be addressed, being more demanding on team time and work. Similarly, negative gossip by staff can mean the work of the team is undermined, can be unfair and shows disrespect, meaning confidence in the team can be undermined. However, such challenges can also galvanise the team to work in a more united fashion. On the other hand, passive subversion is when staff are not doing what they should be doing and getting away with it; it is not helpful and means additional workload can be draining for others.

 Top tip ...

Have clear, up-to-date documentation in place, including accountability measures, to minimise the negative influence of subversion on the team.

6.8 Team behaviours: trust

Trust is a key foundation stone to effective teamwork. Trusting and being trustworthy is key. Beyond 'me' in the team is 'you'. You can only trust that I will continue the teamwork you have done. Being trustworthy as a team player is in turning up every day to work, is in doing your job as expected, and is in being reliable.

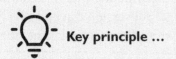

Key principle ...

Trust is a pre-condition for effective teamwork. I can only trust that you will continue the work I have done; 'You' begin where 'I' finish.

Team talk: the parable of the chop sticks

This is an old Zen parable and is very useful when needing to remind the team of the need to work together professionally and trust each other, not to be miscommunicating, gossiping ,or backbiting with each other.

One day in a temple in Tibet, a young Buddhist monk asked his elder 'What is the difference between heaven and hell?' His response was 'They are both the same'. 'How can heaven and hell be both the same?'

'Both are a great room. In the centre of the room is a great table, and on that table is the finest food imaginable, hot and ready to eat. Each person has their own pair of chopsticks with which to eat this fine feast.'

'And so how is one room heaven and one room hell?'

'Because the chopsticks are a metre long. Everyone must use them correctly, holding them from the end. Those in hell continually starve, because they are focused on themselves and cannot reach their mouths with the food in front of them. Those in heaven are continually full, because they understand how to use their chopsticks and feed others across the table with their chopsticks, trusting that in return they will be fed too.'

As a team – we rely on each other to work together.

As others trust in us, we must trust in others.

Whenever possible, develop trust and humour within the team. Trust is a pre-condition for effective teamwork, enables the team to destress in a safe environment, and reduces anxiety. The presence of trust is key to team effectiveness, and its absence, key to team ineffectiveness.

Humour

Interestingly, in the research, there is little cited about the importance of humour in teamwork, yet I am sure we have all experienced the positive influence of having a collective sense of humour when working in a team, however large or small.

In my research, humour came out as an essential component in teamwork and existed when trust was established, and people relaxed into the work with the team of people with whom they were working. One team used WhatsApp for informal communication and humour, keeping the mood between them positive, with fun being important and valued. With a very stressful job, fun can be used to collectively de-stress. Humour is also a way to create more engagement, especially at work and in meetings, and especially with students, where it is an effective way of making learning more engaging.

Top tip ...

Making working together as a team fun cannot be undervalued.

6.9 Team behaviours: balance

Regarding the team's personalities, and with three major studies in this area, if the team is balanced and behaves professionally, the personalities within the team should only have a positive influence on the team. When staff choose not to accept that the team comes before the individual and are unprofessional by being, for example, over-emotional, it can be a negative influence on the team.

Acceptance: help the team understand that in difference is strength

When everybody on the team accepts each other's strengths and weaknesses, they are stronger together, enjoy working together and there is a stronger team bond as a result. Belbin (2010) in his work looked at high-performing teams and put the best brains together in what he called his 'Apollo' team. What he thought would be the best team turned out to be far from it, with competitiveness within the team subverting their success. When members of the team are self-centred or reject that they are stronger together and question the wisdom of working together it means an inability to see the rest of the team outside of themselves. As such, it is incumbent on each member of the team to accept that in difference, and difference of opinion, comes strength. Have a balance of personalities in the team.

Control: distribute leadership between the team rather than hold leadership to yourself

Too much of one personality can be a bad thing (especially that of the headteacher). It is a common trap in teaching that the teacher talks for most of the lesson and hopes the students learn much by noticing the pearls of wisdom being shared. However, we all know that students learn better by engaging with the lesson and owning their own learning. In a similar way, some leaders believe that talking throughout a meeting or sending a myriad of emails is leading a team. To some extent it is, but when that leader leaves, what is left is a vacuum. More effective is what Harris (2013) describes as distributed leadership. In a similar way to the teacher letting go of a lesson empowering students to learn, so the team leader needs to let go of the work of the team for the team to get on and do it.

For example, resolutions created through emotion and pragmatism are thought to be better than when being created through the drive, determination, and belligerence of the team leader. Conversely, whereas emotive responses mean that more time can be taken up in discussions, being emotional, while less than professionally optimal, enables conversations to be covered in more depth.

 Top tip ...

Let the teamwork go for the team to go to work.

6.10 Team behaviours: up-to-date job descriptions, processes, and procedures

Team behaviour can be viewed as a Venn diagram, an influence that is the sum of its individual parts. Efficient teamwork is dependent on everyone playing their part to the full, there being no overlap with the work of other members of the team. Having clear, up-to-date documentation in place to minimise the negative impact of subversion or overlap, able to effectively hold all team players to account is key.

Job descriptions are important to team behaviours in giving direction and clarity. Without them it leaves teamwork more open to misinterpretation.

6.11 Team behaviours: legacies

A further area that emerged from my research was the influence of historic incidents, which could be personal, for example, working for a previously ineffective team, which led to working with initial suspicion with the current team, or organisational, such as inheriting a deficit from the previous regime. All the schools involved in the research referenced examples of organisational legacies that had a negative influence on their work, its influence including historic organisational issues, current team poor practice, and personal experience.

Historic organisational issues

Historic organisational issues provided an opportunity to get to know staff and the school context better but was also an opportunity for staff to close ranks and delay / challenge teamwork.

Historic poor team practice

Historic poor/unclear team practice can sometimes need addressing, creating additional work for the team and increased delays in school improvement. For example, the part of the team that are inherited may be much less inclined to take ownership of their work, due to previous experience of historic poor team practice. This subsequently needs to be successfully addressed.

Historic personal/collective experience

Similarly, historic personal/collective previously successful experience meant outdated, anachronistic expectations from staff of their students, with occasional historic previous experience/expertise being able to be drawn on today.

Thus, previous personal experience of organisational or team past failure creates a lack of confidence in the team or team leadership, experienced as scepticism or reticence from the team. For example, team members saying 'Yes, but when the previous Head of Department did that ...', showing agreement, but potentially putting historic blocks in the way, in a similar way to 'That didn't work then, and won't work now'. Be ready with 'That was then and this is now', or 'let's unpack what the issues were and ensure it works better this time'. Either way:

 Top tip ...

Do not let past team failures influence future team success.

6.12 Team behaviours: summary

Key ingredient three: behaviours – building team relationships

Influence on the team: increasing helpful behaviours
Impact: increasing positive team relationships

Key takeaways	Key messages
To improve the effectiveness of the team, identify behaviours that are ineffective, specify actions that need to improve, and raise the expectations that have been set.	• Expectations clarify actions; repeated actions become behaviours; behaviours produce effective or ineffective working.
Expect support, honesty, openness, respect, and trust from every team member as they are the key foundation stones to effective teamwork.	• Without the basics being in place, for any team, of support, honesty, openness, respect and trust, the team will go nowhere.
Support: expect the team to be there for each other, putting the 'we' before 'me'.	• Team ethos: support is a given. • Collective acceptance: we support everyone in the team, whatever their foibles. • As a team be pragmatic. Like a Swiss Army knife, the team uses its diverse skills, knowledge, and qualities to successfully tackle any issue. • Praise in public; criticise in private. • Peer pressure: do not let the side down. • Team loyalty: above all else, be loyal.
Be honest: honesty really is the best policy. Be open, with each other and to the new; but not to the detriment of the team.	• Being honest with each other gets to the heart of any issue (and therefore any solution) quickly. • Be open to new ideas and initiatives but be careful not to say 'yes' to everything.

Continued on next page

Key takeaways	Key messages
Be respectful and professional at all times.	• Manage team issues quickly and nip them in the bud. As much as possible, the team's time and energy should be focused on delivering high quality teaching and learning; nothing else. • Have clear, up-to-date documentation in place, including accountability measures, to minimise the negative influence of subversion on the team.
Trust: whenever possible, develop trust and humour within the team.	• Trust is a pre-condition for effective teamwork; I can only trust that you will continue the work I have done; 'You' begin where 'I' finish. • Making working together as a team fun cannot be undervalued.
Balance: have a balance of personalities in the team.	• Acceptance: help the team understand that in difference is strength. • Control: distribute leadership between the team rather than hold leadership to yourself. • Let the teamwork go for the team to go to work.

➢ Team behaviours: have up-to-date job descriptions/processes and procedures.

➢ Legacy: do not let past personal or team failures influence future team success.

7 Key ingredient 4: infrastructures – ensuring team functionality

Influence on the team: improving processes and procedures

Impact: increasing team functionality/effectiveness

7.1 Introduction

A transparent and functional infrastructure is beneficial both to a team and the school. This chapter provides clarification as to what we mean by infrastructure, the influence and impact on the team and others when we get our team infrastructure right, and when we get our team infrastructure wrong. It unpacks in more detail the importance of efficient meetings, robust decision-making, effective time and workload management, improved work/life balance, and strong leadership. It offers a checklist to help audit a team in relation to their infrastructure and offers case studies and strategies to develop and improve this further.

7.2 Audit: team infrastructure

To clarify the extent to which your team or school's infrastructures are in place and working well, consider completing this short audit, either by yourself or with the rest of the team/school. Once completed, you will be able to identify the team infrastructures that require immediate action (infrastructures that need to be in place/need urgent revision), infrastructures that require short-term action (infrastructures that need tweaking/need to be more consistent), or which require medium-term action, identifying the team's/school's next steps. The following infrastructures are not exhaustive. Tweak or change as needed!

DOI: 10.4324/9781003303404-7

Team infrastructure audit	Positive measure	In place working well	In place needs tweaking	In place needs much work	Not in place	Negative measure
Budget management	Strong					Weak
Decision-making	Strong					Weak
Key documentation	All in place/ up to date					Not in place/ out of date
Leadership	Strong					Weak
Meetings	Well-led					Poorly led
Processes/ procedures	Clear/all comply					Unclear/none comply
Staffing	Sufficient					Insufficient
Workload	Manageable					Unmanageable

Follow up:

Immediate action (expectations need to be in place/need urgent revision):

Short-term action (need tweaking/need to be more consistent):

Medium-term action (identify next steps):

7.3 Empowering and enabling team leadership

Distributed leadership can be viewed as a positive influence, responsibility being devolved to the team that enables the work of the school to be more efficiently and effectively performed. However, this can come at a price, as it can create additional work and stress when team members do not do their share of the work, due to absence or other reasons (e.g. an urgent student or staff issue). This situation can be exacerbated by the omission or lack of clarity of job descriptions. Thus, when team leadership is going well, the team should be happy to follow that lead. However, when the team leader is absent, otherwise engaged or distracted, the team should feel comfortable to step in and take the lead.

With any team, staff, including the team leader, are going to be absent. It happens. An occasional day here are then can be managed. The issue is when the occasional day becomes a week and when the occasional week becomes a month. As team leaders we usually look for the best in people and we cope. However, this is one area in which it is advisable to not cope. If a member of staff is absent, always get cover, however bad or however inconvenient this is. At the end of the day, work needs to be done by someone. Not getting in cover means someone has to do double the work. If the person covering does not have the expertise of the people absent, what did you do to prepare for this?

It is essential for team leaders to always have a plan B for every member of the team. If the cover supervisor is off, who steps in and knows what to do? If the bursar is absent, who can step in and run the school's finances in their absence? This issue is exacerbated with the size of the team: the smaller the team, the bigger the impact of staff absence. Thus it is more important for people who run small teams to always have a plan B.

Top tip ...

The smaller the team, the bigger the impact of staff absence. Always know who will step in when others are absent.

Team talk: empowering, enabling leadership always has a plan B

In any team, the team leader may be the best of a bad bunch, which means they will not be the best team leader, may have a significant life crisis, which means they will not be the best team leader for a significant amount of time, or may be missing a particular skill set, which means the team are not able to develop as quickly as they might otherwise do.

In the first scenario, when the team leader is not the best, and the team leader does not empower the team as well as they could do, it is down to the rest of the team to cover, enable the team to take over, and ensure that the team work effectively, despite not having the best leadership at the top. I have been part of a number of teams where deputy headteachers have effectively been the headteacher or where the second in department has effectively (in both senses of the word) been the Head of Department.

In the second scenario, when the team leader (or any member of staff with sole responsibility for a key area of school life) has a crisis, it is essential that there is a plan B should they be absent. This means setting up Continuing Professional Development (CPD) for other staff who can effectively step into their role should the need arise. This is most clearly shown in the role of deputy headteacher, for when the headteacher is absent. However, this should also be in place when any Senior Leadership Team (SLT) colleague, the SENDCO, timetabler, cover supervisor, premises team and exams officer (to name a few) are absent.

In the third scenario, where a team leader does not utilise a key skill with the team (for example, using social media or using online technology), this needs to be discussed openly within the team and a way forward agreed. I have worked with a number of school leaders where technology was not for them, and their work was always completed on paper (and then typed up by someone else later) or they preferred to use paper diaries

Continued on next page

rather than moving to an outlook calendar, which could be easily shared with the rest of the team. In these scenarios, it was up to the team to either work around this (themselves taking electronic notes of the minutes, rather than on paper) or agreeing to run a centralised online diary, to which the team leader had access. This situation is not ideal and needs careful handling, as the team leader needs to accept that on one aspect of team leadership, the team are leading!

 Top tip ...

Distribute leadership, responsibility being devolved to the team enables the work of the school to be more efficiently and effectively performed.

7.4 Team leadership: as player, leader, and manager

When researching this area, an interesting point emerged. Team leaders, and especially headteachers, are in a unique position. All are part of a team and as such can be regarded as equals to the rest of the team, as team players. All team leaders are likely to be successful at being team players as this is a known role they would have experienced previously. Similarly, they are a team leader because they have some form of expertise or specialism, some quality that marks them out as more of a leader than others in the team. As all team leaders would have been through an interview process, all team leaders are likely to be successful in leading their team. Where the team leader role gets messy, especially as a headteacher, is in a third aspect to the role and that is as team manager or employer. This takes the team leader into unchartered territory (employment rights, human resources, and finances, to name three), which in the hands of less adept team leaders may not be handled as deftly as other team leadership roles.

In relation to the leadership of the team, leader centricity can be mixed in its influence on the team. Indeed, from my own professional experience, I have experienced first-hand the havoc created by team leaders who are not as emotionally intelligent or as adept as leaders as they could be, making teamwork less effective as a result. In my research, the ability of the team leader to effectively manage their role as 'team manager' was particularly contentious, the influence of the team leader being both positive and negative. The positive influences included the collaboration, collegiality, consistency, and confidence of the leadership and the public perception of the success of that leadership. The small number of responses that were negative related to the team leader not managing well and excessive team leader or governor support meant challenge was not always as effective as it could be.

The consistency and confidence of the team leader as team leader helped prioritise the right work for the team and helped model/make things happen in the right order at the right time in the right way, whereas leadership change/absence meant a change in strategic direction/priorities and put a strain on team, while the overconfidence of the team leader or members of the team could be controlling, upsetting, or destructive. Similarly, the confidence of the team leader as a strong team leader helped the team be aligned politically and deliver Ofsted success; however, a very close working relationship between the team leader and their seniors to the exclusion of the team, was viewed as unhealthy.

 Top tip ...

The influence of the team leader as team player or team leader is usually a positive one; as team manager, beware potential problems.

7.5 Team processes and procedures

When structures/systems are in place, this supports better staff and pupil behaviour and more effective teamwork as a result. However, when systems were not in place/needed building, it meant less effective teamwork and a less effective school. In addition, when structures were not in place but then put in place, it had a positive influence because teamwork was more effective, whereas structures that were in place but weak, had a negative influence and meant the work of the team was not as effective. Have clear, up-to-date development plan, calendar, policies, job descriptions, and staff handbook, so all processes and procedures can flow as easily as possible.

This is especially true for duties. The bane of most staff's job, however, after teaching or their main role, it is the most important. Everyone doing their duty means a stronger sense of team cohesion. It also means that what needs to get done, is done, the team not dropping the ball (nor the school if all teams do what is expected of them).

When teams carry out their duties it means the school community can carry on with their own work without worry or concern. However, if there is an expectation to be available all the time for duties it can mean prioritising duties over other work, thus demanding more time than may be available. Moreover, dealing with issues from duties can sometimes take away time and adds to the team's workload. It is essential that duties are clear and staffed sufficiently to secure operational effectiveness but are not so thin that breakdowns in operational effectiveness occur or so heavy as to take staff away from carrying out their main roles.

Top tip ...

Have processes and procedures in black and white. These can be followed explicitly. When there is a shade of grey, expect confusion, misinterpretation, and ineffective teamwork.

7.6 Meetings and briefings

Meetings: enable everyone in the community to feel supported

How many meetings have you sat in that have, to a greater or lesser degree, been a waste of time? On the other side, how many meetings have you sat in where things have been run efficiently and lots of decisions have been made and good work has been done?

The right number of meetings confirms sufficient workload and efficiently uses time; however, too many meetings increases workload by diminishing time to do existing work and usually creates work. Indeed, inflexible meeting times and agendas were seen as less effective when being unresponsive to variable workloads. Meetings are where the working consciousness of an organisation comes together to review, discuss, decide, and plan. It is therefore essential for the organisation that there are enough meetings with the right people to do this effectively but not so many that no one has the time to action the outcome of the meetings.

Top tip ...

Decide the meetings you want to have with the various teams (students, staff, leaders, parents, and governors) and agree their membership, frequency, and purpose.

Meetings are meant to be supportive, aiding workload management and ownership as well as being a conduit of communication within the team. Meetings enabled the team to be supportive of each other and mean, subsequently, improved leadership. These type of meetings typically include weekly SLT meetings, fortnightly line management meetings, and monthly leadership meetings. Meetings create a sense of shared ownership or teamwork.

Meetings are one of the main conduits of communication, enabling the team to communicate meaningfully, formally, and informally, with what is important, and facilitate a decrease in workload; however, the important work of the school being discussed at meetings means these could be repetitive, long and increase team workload. Communication in meetings also enables the existence of a collective awareness, which means that all team members are aware of the positive and negative things happening in school; yet, this also means more voices around the table, taking up time in discussion rather than action. In addition, communication in meetings ensures that decisions made are as good as they can be; sometimes, meetings can get side-tracked and therefore the decisions are not as good as they could be.

Meetings: line management effectively supports and hold leaders to account

When a line management structure is followed, it can mean less work for the team, which also facilitates effective communication and support, minimising dissent and nipping issues in the bud. All staff should have some form of accountability for their work, directly or indirectly tied to the achievement and progress of students. Leaders' work especially should be measured against this standard, with clear milestones to be reached to show that we are on track to meet our targets and where this is not the case, what different actions are going to be taken to move things sufficiently forward.

 Top tip ...

Ensure meetings enable both accountability (To what extent are we on track to meet our targets?) and support (What needs to be done differently to ensure we meet or exceed our targets?) to sufficiently move things forward.

Briefings: short daily briefings enable teamwork to be effectively responsive

My research concurred with other research in relation to structures and the benefit of having clear structures in place, including duties and meetings, which provide support, facilitate communication, and promote ownership of the work. A key recommendation from the schools taking part in the research was in the importance of a daily briefing at the start of the day, which helped teams, especially leadership teams, be as responsive, and thus as effective, as they practically could be.

7.7 Decision-making

A further key aspect of the infrastructure for effective teamwork is the importance of effective decision-making and the role of the team leader in this. Teamwork can be viewed as being effective when decisions made are collective, with the team leader being open to the input of others in their decision-making. This helps improve public perception of the team and the school, where there is explicit collaboration and collegiality, consistency, and confidence in the decision-making process.

Openness

When the team leader or team are open and able to listen to dissenting views or are flexible/adaptable in their decision-making, it means better decisions are made. Equally, worse decisions are made by individuals who are not open to others' views (e.g. at interview), which creates clashes and, subsequently, has negative ramifications.

Collective decision-making

Collective decision-making means more considered decisions can be made. However, with more people being involved it can mean less time to make collective decisions, meaning less considered decisions can be made. Moreover, whereas better/faster decisions are made by teams from managing and listening to others' views, drawing on others' experience/expertise enables all to feel positive and included. Yet, when poor decisions are made, this can lead to tensions between the team, leading to disagreement/low morale and increased worry within the team and leaders having to manage the emotional fall out.

Checked decision-making

A variation to the collective decision-making is where the decision made by an individual is checked by others (other team member/s, the team leader, or governors). This can be helpful in checking and ensuring decisions made are agreeable and achievable. Where decisions are made autonomously, are unaligned with the school's improvement trajectory, and go unchecked, it can cause issues and upset. Thus, ensure decision-making processes within the team are clear and, where needed, collaboration takes place.

 Top tip ...

Ensure decision-making processes within the team are clear and, where needed, collaboration takes place.

7.8 Communication

The COVID-19 pandemic has had a revolutionary effect on communication across the globe. More than ever before we are able to communicate with each other, anytime and anywhere that has an internet connection. Most people will be up-to-speed with the following. Ensure your team and your school are fully operational with each of these ten classic ways of working online as a team.

Ten top online tools for teams

Efficient meeting set-up: Outlook Calendar:

1. Keep your work diary electronically and invite as many colleagues as you like to a meeting.

2. Keep your work diary electronically and share it with as many colleagues as you like so your meetings can be set up without double booking each other.

    Efficient meetings: MS Teams or Zoom

3. Use Teams or Zoom to ensure that people who are not able to be present physically can be present to a meeting virtually. This works especially well for parent meetings.

4. Record meetings on Teams or Zoom to keep a record of the meeting or send to others at a later date.

5. Use the Whiteboard function in Teams or Zoom to capture discussions.

    Efficient communication: Outlook emails

6. Cc or bcc in the people that need to know to any email exchange.

7. Set up email groups to save time sending an email to multiple people.

8. For large groups, set up a spreadsheet and enable leaders to mail merge documents.

    Efficient editing: Word/Google Docs

9. Set up a document on a shared area and allow others to co-edit, comment or see it.

10. Use the Review/Comment facility online to give concurrent feedback on work requiring feedback.

Top tip ...

Have a clear communications policy that promotes the efficient and effective use by teams of social media, email, and other online programmes

7.9 Workload

The work of most teams in school can seem like a hamster wheel as each week rolls into the next, and the demands of staff, students, and parents continues unabated, meaning the team having to work long hours (including working after hours at home), with a negative impact on home life. This can also impact the team's ability to do their work effectively. Having a sense of unrelenting work can also create pressure points for the team during the year, especially when meeting times are inflexible. However, having to prioritise the important work of the team means a sense of essential work getting completed.

Team size: understand the influence of team size on your team's workload

A smaller team means a broader workload/more generalist work because there are fewer people to complete the work. A larger team means a narrower workload/ more specialist work since there are more people to complete the work.

Work expectations: ensure work expectations are clear

Clear and focused roles/expectations are helpful in clarifying necessary work, whereas disingenuous expectations of work are not helpful and means higher frustration.

Communication: communicate frequently but not to the detriment of team mental health

Frequent communication, especially through social media/emails can be demanding and increase the workload of the team, and being screen-based means being physically tied to a computer in the office, reducing visibility around school.

Relying on others: beware!

Reliance on others to do their work, which is then out of team control, has a negative impact when not done, not done on time, and is followed with an unfair judgement by others on the team.

Top tip ...

Have a clear workload policy that promotes the effective use by teams of efficient working practices.

7.10 Team infrastructure: summary

Key ingredient four: infrastructure – ensuring team functionality

Influence on the team: improving processes and procedures
Impact: Increasing team functionality/effectiveness

Key takeaways	Key messages
Leadership: when the team leader is leading well – be happy to follow. When the team leader is not leading well – be happy to lead.	• Distribute leadership, responsibility being devolved to the team enables the work of the school to be more efficiently and effectively performed.
Team leadership: as team player, great; as team leader, great; as team manager, beware potential problems.	• The influence of the team leader as team player or team leader is usually a positive one; as team manager, beware potential problems.
Have a clear, up-to-date development plan, calendar, policies, job descriptions, and staff handbook, so all processes and procedures can flow as easily as possible.	• Have processes and procedures in black and white. These can be followed explicitly. When there is a shade of grey, you are lost.
Staffing: hope for the best but prepare for the worst. Always have a plan B.	• The smaller the team, the bigger the impact of staff absence. Always know who will step in when others are absent.

Continued on next page

Key takeaways	Key messages
Duties: ensure duties are clear and staffed sufficiently to secure operational effectiveness.	• Ensure duties are clear and staffed sufficiently to secure operational effectiveness but are not so thin that breakdowns in operational effectiveness occur or so heavy as to take staff away from carrying out their main roles.
Meetings: ensure meetings enable both accountability and support.	• Decide the meetings you want to have with the various teams (students, staff, leaders, parents, and governors) and agree their membership, frequency, and purpose. • Ensure meetings enable both accountability (To what extent are we on track to meet our targets?) and support (What needs to be done differently to ensure we meet or exceed our targets?) to sufficiently move things forward.
Briefings: have a short daily briefing to keep the work of the team as responsive to events as possible.	• Have a daily briefing at the start of the day, which helped teams, especially leadership teams, be as responsive, and thus as effective, as they practically can be.
Decisions: ensure decision-making processes within the team are clear and collaboration where needed takes place.	• Ensure decisions made are open and transparent, are as collaborative as possible, and checked, to ensure internal or external validity.
Communicate smartly: have a clear communications policy that promotes the effective use by teams of social media, email, and online programmes.	*Ten top online tools for teams* 1. Keep your work diary electronically and invite as many colleagues as you like to a meeting. 2. Keep your work diary electronically and share it with as many colleagues as you like so your meetings can be set up without double booking each other. 3. Use Teams or Zoom to ensure that people who are not able to be present physically can be present to a meeting virtually. This works especially well for parent meetings. 4. Record meetings on Teams or Zoom to keep a record of the meeting or send to others at a later date. 5. Use the Whiteboard function in Teams or Zoom to capture discussions

Continued on next page

Key takeaways	Key messages
	6. Cc or bcc in the people that need to know to any email exchange.
	7. Set up email groups to save time sending an email to multiple people.
	8. For large groups, set up a spreadsheet and enable leaders to mail merge documents.
	9. Set up a document on a shared area and allow others to co-edit, comment or see it.
	10. Use the Review/Comment facility online to give concurrent feedback on work requiring feedback.
Work smartly: have a clear workload policy that promotes the effective use by teams of efficient working practices.	• 'If you always do what you've always done, you'll always get what you've always got.' (Henry Ford)

8 Key ingredient 5: capacity – developing team growth

Influence on the team: increasing available provision
Impact: increasing team capacity to deliver goals

8.1 Introduction

This chapter provides clarification as to what we mean by capacity, the influence and impact on the team and others when we develop our capacity in the right way and what happens when we do not. It unpacks in more detail the importance of team expertise, innovation, quality assurance, constructive criticism, and staff development. It offers a checklist to help audit a team in relation to their capacity for growth and offers case studies and strategies to develop and improve this further.

When we talk about capacity, we are talking about the ability for the team to support and improve itself; to keep up-to-date and effective; to weather staff absence and the trials and tribulations of the everyday, without losing momentum. This specifically means the extent to which a team understands the potential it has within it: the experienced experts that are happy and able to coach and mentor the less experienced; the new, innovative member of the team who is happy to get everyone up-to-speed with the latest technological advances in education; the member of the team who is always difficult, but who is fully committed and just needs a more constructive role within the team to be recognised and more fulfilled. Below are six ways we can improve the work of the team through working on the team's capacity to improve.

8.2 Audit: team capacity

To clarify the extent to which your team or school's capacity to improve is in place and working well, consider completing this short audit, either by yourself or with

DOI: 10.4324/9781003303404-8

the rest of the team/school. Once completed, you will be able to identify the team's capacity to improve that requires immediate action (capacity that needs to be in place/needs urgent revision); capacity that requires short-term action (capacity that needs tweaking/needs to be more consistent); or which requires medium-term action, identifying the team's/school's next steps. The following ideas are not exhaustive. Tweak or change as needed!

Team capacity audit	Positive measure	In place working well	In place needs tweaking	In place needs much work	Not in place	Negative measure
Budget	Efficiently spent					Inefficiently spent
CPD	Well trained					Untrained
CPD opportunities	Taken					Missed
Expertise	Mobilised					Untapped
Innovation	Considered/ implemented					Unconsidered/ not implemented
Mindset	Open					Closed
Professional practice	Best-practice					Sub-optimal
Technology	Efficiently used					Inefficiently used

Follow up:

Immediate action (expectations need to be in place/need urgent revision):

Short-term action (need tweaking/need to be more consistent):

Medium-term action (identify next steps):

8.3 Improving capacity: from micro to macro influence

Sharing best practice: teaching and learning

When we work in a school, no one works as an island. Everything we do influences and affects the degree to which students successfully learn. Therefore, when we are working individually or in a team and identify a solution to a problem others maybe facing, the school should have a mechanism whereby staff are able to share their individual or team success and solutions and enable others to do the same.

Team talk: seven things to do to share best practice

- Have a suggestion box at reception.
- Have a 'You said – we did' section on the weekly staff bulletin.
- Have a 'Sharing Best Practice' slot at department and staff meetings.
- Host department meetings/team meetings in different areas of the school.
- Have staff lead CPD sessions in areas they are expert/have outstanding work.
- Work with universities/Teaching School Alliances (TSAs) and access latest teaching innovations through trainee teachers.
- Work with universities and TSAs to be involved with latest educational research.

 Top tip ...

Have a suggestion box, a 'top tips' item at department or staff meetings for staff to share good practice, and ensure there is more consistent good practice between the team and the school.

Increasing finances

In my research, limited finances were a major impediment to teamwork. Limited finances meant team choices were limited, tensions arose as to how best to manage things, and school improvement slowed, which stifled enjoyment and dampened the working atmosphere. In addition, financial limitations stifled creativity, but, paradoxically, encouraged innovation and creativity; for example, enabling staff to work part-time increased ability to effectively staff the school and meant a decreased workload for the team as a result.

Similarly, reduced lettings, managing a deficit budget, or having fewer students attending the school meant a reduction in school finances, which meant increased staff workload, fewer choices, and limited long-term school improvement. Moreover, reduced finances meant reduced staffing, which for the team meant an increased danger of safeguarding issues, impacting negatively on staff (and hence the team), and previously completed work was wasted. Where income was increased, a broader curriculum was able to be offered, which also positively impacted the school roll, meaning increased income. Conversely, the need to restrict curriculum choice, negatively impacted pupil choice and meant a reduction in the school roll and, as a result, less money.

This is supported in that when the school roll is full, finances are secure, which feels good for the team; however, when the roll drops and is not full, there is less money, and this is a major focus for the team to take more students, creating more work, tension, and high pressure between groups within the school as it is everyone's responsibility, and everyone has conflicting ways to increase the school roll. Thus, when looking to implement improvements, seek first to improve how we work as an organisation, then how we work as a team, then how we work as individuals.

Team talk: seven things to do to increase income

- Improve relationships with primary schools and increase the school roll.
- Improve relationships with the community and increase lettings.
- Work with universities and TSAs to increase the number of trainee teachers.
- Work with universities and TSAs to increase school involvement with funded research.
- Reduce staff absence through rigorously applying staff wellbeing and staff absence policies.
- Employ cover supervisors rather than having supply teachers.
- Apply for all relevant funding opportunities with the DfE or LEA that arise.

8.4 Managing change

'The only three things that are certain in life are death, taxes and change.' Few schools move from one academic year to the next without some change in staffing, certainly a change in students as Year 11 and Year 13 leave, and the Year 6 students become the new Year 7. Thus, there is built into the school year that change in personnel. Other changes may be necessary depending on the school's need to spend or save money, or to develop a key priority. All this requires change and therefore the need for team leaders to manage that change.

In my previous book, *The School Leader's Year*, the months of June, July, and September are months of high workload pressure for school leaders, which makes implementing any changes problematic in that any change may not necessarily get the time and attention it might need. As a result, I recommend consulting on changes in April and May, with tweaks to any changes being implemented in July for implementation at the start of the school year (and therefore staff being aware of the changes that are being implemented).

Two changes that teams need to manage include changes in day-to-day workload and changes in staffing/responsibilities. Two models to help the team be aware and help manage these changes are Eisenhower's Matrix and Tuckman's stages of group development.

Helping prioritise the team's day-to-day work: Eisenhower's Matrix

Time and energy are the two key resources we all need to protect as much as we possibly can, so we can accomplish the work we need to do effectively. Amending this classic leadership matrix for the team, the table below helps a team prioritise their work.

	Urgent	**Not urgent**
Important	*DO* *Do it now*	*DECIDE* *Schedule a time to do it*
Not important	*DELEGATE / SHARE* *Who can do it for you / with you*	*DELETE* *Eliminate it*

DO: If the work in hand is important and urgent, this needs to be done straight away by you and no one else. Time, whatever it takes, is a must. For example, preparing work for lessons that need to be taught today or preparing resources for a meeting later in the day. All other work must wait.

DECIDE: It is better to look at the diary for the week ahead and schedule in time to work on what needs to be done later in the week. This enables you to give sufficient time for the work in hand and to draw on others' expertise/work if needed.

DELEGATE/SHARE: If the work is urgent – but others can do the work as much as you – ask others to help. For example, if you have an urgent, important meeting and need a duty covering, asking a colleague to cover (obviously returning the favour, later, when needed), will ensure the urgent and less important gets done just as much as the urgent and important. Similarly, if others are teaching the same year group or have similar meetings (e.g. Heads of Year preparing this week's assembly), one could prepare a template for others to use, saving the team precious time.

Finally, understanding what is important to the team's work helps making the decision to delete unwanted emails, calls etc., and helps decrease unnecessary work and maintain team focus on what is important and necessary.

Helping manage changes in staff/responsibilities: Tuckman's stages of group development

A classic piece of research to help manage changes in staffing or responsibilities within the team is Tuckman's stages of group development. He identified four stages of development as the team settles and gets used to working together.

Forming: As the team begin to work together, the team are not as effective as they could be as team relationships are developing and new staff get used to the team's ethos and ways of working. Time and effort are best invested in making connections and ensuring that everything that needs to be done is done.

Storming: As the team get used to their roles and are increasingly confident and challenging, relationships become more difficult. This is a normal part of the change process. Time and effort are best invested in clarifying any confusion or sorting any miscommunication or misunderstandings.

Norming: Having worked through any misunderstandings or miscommunication, the team become more trusting with each other, each member of the team becoming more reliable and delivering on their part of the teamwork. As a result, time and effort are best invested in recognising good practice and reinforcing and inconsistencies or weaknesses.

Performing: With major upsets being resolved and strengths within the team emerging and inconsistencies being resolved, the team emerge as performing, everyone effectively contributing their part to the team's whole. Time and effort are best spent celebrating success, developing team strengths, and reinforcing best practice.

With any staffing changes, being aware of this process and supporting the team to move through it as quickly as possible will help the team manage change as effectively as possible and ensure that time and energy are effectively spent on the work in hand.

 Top tip ...

Use a suitable change management model to ensure when change is needed, the team successfully manages the process.

8.5 Team CPD

It is clear that while there is plenty of CPD for individual team members and team leaders within schools, there is very little CPD for teams.

Effective CPD for team members, team leaders, and teams included mentoring, coaching, and awaydays. This included the more well-trained staff/team sharing what they had learnt, as the more well-trained the team were, the more effective they were, and conversely, a newer/less well-trained staff/team meant the team were less effective.

Drach-Zahavy and Somech's (2001, p. 121) research, recommended that teams 'make deliberate efforts and engage in team building and training interventions to learn how to work (more effectively) together'. However, this needs to be scheduled as part of staff development. Further research in this area would be beneficial as to how much time is scheduled and used for staff development as opposed to team development and, equally, individual development as opposed to team development.

The key issue for teams in schools is in managing more pressing priorities. These more pressing priorities mean that the team's CPD does not happen and thus the team are not as developed as they could be. Thus, it is important for team leaders to make time in department, SLT or year team meetings to ensure the team have time set aside to help them develop as a team. As one of the participants in the research observed:

> More communication would be helpful, you know, because if we had a greater awareness, you know, it's like that thing, if you don't use it, you forget it, unless you're working in an area and they're off, and if they're not there; hopefully between us, we can probably do enough together to manage. I think the idea of everyone being trained on different areas and all that (is good), the biggest barrier to that is money and time ...

 **Top tip ...**

Spend just as much time developing the team as well as developing the individual: CPD should not just be focused on 'How much better can I work?' but also 'How much better can we work together?'

8.6 Innovation

Themes from my research that also helped developed team capacity was in the team's ability to be open to new ideas and new ways of doing things. This is encapsulated well in Carol Dweck's revolutionary work, which clearly shows the important link between being open to the new and being successful.

New ideas introduced to the team are found to be helpful in that they help stop poor practice developing, which means a new way of doing things and thus the possibility of improving the team's current practice. However, new ideas are also destabilising, which means challenges occurs when looking to improve current team practice for example, from one research participant:

> It's kind of like having a new puppy, kind of like every other week, and I just want us to grow up, we just tend to lose our way, and it's great to have

enthusiasm, and it's great to have all these 'Wow! wow! wow!', and it's fantastic, but fundamentally, what is our core product, you know? And there aren't 100 ways to produce that?

A key time for teams to capitalise on new ideas and new ways of doing things is when new staff join the team and offer an opportunity to bring new ideas, new technologies, and be the proverbial 'breath of fresh air'. New staff bring new energy, which means the increased possibility of improving current team practice. New technologies enable teamwork to be more effective.

Top tip ...

Routinely discuss innovative practice within the team, sharing ideas and best practice.

8.7 Team expertise

Expertise can be shown in how well the team leader understands how their group is developing into a credible, performing team and ensures that this happens. The findings in my research concurred with the literature in that this emphasis on the value of experts in the team, who are more likely to bring stability, experience, and strong skills to the team than would otherwise apply. However, this was not without its challenges, where the more expert staff could be more challenging and demanding than other staff, with their skills sets being less easy to replace if they were absent.

In particular, having a breadth of expertise within the team and understanding those skills contributed positively to the team, the student experience, and the school and meant more effective teamwork in moving the school forward. However, the absence of/less experience/mismatch of expertise in the role meant the team was less effective and different skills within the team, which were too niche, meant more work and less effective teamwork in helping move the school forward.

Longevity: Being kept in a role embeds and develops expertise, especially when the expertise of staff matches the current and future needs of the school; however, when someone leaves or the post is removed, the specialism can be challenging to replace.

Exclusivity: Being an expert creates an exclusivity and creates a member of staff who is demanding/has a higher sense of entitlement than others, which means they are more likely to be a non-team player, creating more work for the team; however, being an expert creates an exclusivity in one's field and a unique awareness of one's contribution/support to the team. For example, from one participant, 'I think that where you have someone who's responsible for something that no one else is responsible for, obviously, you've got issues if they then leave.'

Similarly, not being an expert/skilled means additional work to learn those skills/ time spent supporting others; however, being an expert enabled team members to defend their brief effectively.

Highly experienced staff/governors were likely to be more challenging, cynical, and difficult/prejudiced about new ideas for school improvement.

Modesty: Some of the team who were particularly modest meant they did not celebrate their success in that role as much as they could have done.

Expertise of the team leader: Where there was a lack of seniority, especially in the role of the team leader, this impacted negatively on the confidence of the team:

Top tip ...

Use and deploy the expertise in your team to the team's advantage.

8.8 Team capacity: summary

Key ingredient five: capacity – ensuring team functionality

Influence on the team: improving processes and procedures
Impact: increasing team functionality/effectiveness

Key takeaways	Key messages
Improving capacity: from micro to macro influence	• Have a suggestion box, a 'top tips' item at department or staff meetings for staff to share good practice and ensure there is more consistent good practice between the team and the school.
	Seven things to do to share best practice
	• Have a suggestion box at reception.
	• Have a 'You said – we did' section on the weekly staff bulletin.
	• Have a 'Sharing Best Practice' slot at department and staff meetings.
	• Host department meetings/team meetings in different areas of the school.
	• Have staff lead CPD sessions in areas they are expert/have outstanding work.

Continued on next page

Key takeaways	Key messages
	• Work with universities/TSAs and access latest teaching innovations through trainee teachers.
	• Work with universities and TSAs to be involved with latest educational research.
	Seven things to do to increase income
	• Improve relationships with primary schools and increase the school roll.
	• Improve relationships with the community and increase lettings.
	• Work with universities and TSAs to increase the number of trainee teachers.
	• Work with universities and TSAs to increase school involvement with funded research.
	• Reduce staff absence through rigorously applying staff wellbeing and staff absence policies.
	• Employ cover supervisors rather than having supply teachers.
	• Apply for all relevant funding opportunities with the DfE or LEA which arise.
Managing change	• Use a suitable change management model to ensure when change is needed, the team successfully manages the process. E.g. Help prioritise the team's day-to-day work using Eisenhower's Matrix or help manage changes in staff/responsibilities using Tuckman's stages of group development.
Team CPD	• Spend just as much time developing the team as well as developing the individual: CPD should not just be focused on 'How much better can I work?', but also 'How much better can we work together?'
Innovation	• Routinely discuss innovative practice within the team, sharing ideas and best practice.
Team expertise	• Use and deploy the expertise in your team to the team's advantage.

Emerging factors from research influencing effective teamwork

9.1 Team balance: introduction

Outlines the most recent writing and research on effective teamwork, both in education and in business to give a comprehensive, up-to-date review of best practice in the field. It unpacks the factors that have a positive influence to be promoted (e.g. trust), factors with a negative influence to be minimised (e.g. subversion), and factors with both a positive and negative influence to be managed (e.g. communication). The chapter concludes with the factors which positively, negatively and both positively and negatively influence effective teamwork in schools according to my research.

9.2 Team balance: internal factor/positive influence

For a team to work effectively, it needs to be 'in balance' (Belbin, 2010, p. 107). An imbalance in representation creates an imbalance in effectiveness. Thus, a factor influencing the effective work of a team is maintaining team heterogeneity. This suggests that for the leader and the team, they should be aware of the balance within the team and lead/manage the team accordingly (Maier, 1971; Bantel and Jackson, 1989; Drach-Zahavy and Somech, 2001).

In creating a team, it is important to have the key 'attributes' (Hall, 2002). While it may at first seem important to have the best brains and talent around the table, Belbin (2010, p. 23) found that having what he terms the 'Apollo' team (best of brains) regularly came last in team challenges. In other words, a group of talented individuals do not necessarily make a great team (Goleman et al., 2002; Hall, 2002). This was because working at such a high level of criticality or fault-finding, they applied this to both their work and themselves, 'bringing a constructive energy to the table, but a destructive energy to the team' (Belbin, 2010, p. 23). In addition, Neumann (1991), in her study on group composition and effective team roles, found that administrative team members thought in terms of eight prototypical roles/ clusters: the definer, the analyst, the interpreter, the critic, the synthesiser, the disparity monitor, the task monitor, and the emotional monitor. The study

DOI: 10.4324/9781003303404-9

concluded that the degree of cognitive role differentiation in the configuration of a team, 'made a significant contribution to the effectiveness of the team's work' (Neumann, 1991, p. 510). That is, cognitively diverse teams are more likely to be more effective than those that are not.

In managing any team, it is important to minimise the negative and encourage the positive. The seminal work by Belbin found that to maximise positive team dynamics, roles should be complementary, with a strong 'chair' and the existence of 'implementer' and 'plant' roles within the team (Belbin, 2010). Further positive influences include member contribution, adaptability, timing, flexibility, and self-restraint (Riaz and Sultan, 2017). In contrast, where there were role clashes, role voids, role overlaps, high levels of competition, or several personalities that had similar strengths or weaknesses within the team, these were negative influences that needed to be managed (Belbin, 2010). Furthermore, Belbin determined that their mental ability was an important factor and the selection process a significant factor on the effectiveness of the team (Hall, 2002). Effective teams, therefore, are balanced and have an optimal size. Belbin (2010, p.116) recommends that the optimal size of a team for it to be effective has between 3 and 12 members. The larger the team, the poorer the team processes (Currall et al., 2001; Belbin, 2010). Thus, the research suggests that having a balanced team, optimally comprising no more than 6 or 7 people, working professionally together, helps teamwork be more effective.

 Top tip ...

Ensure there is a balance of personalities, skills, and personal qualities within a team.

9.3 Team balance: collaboration

Schools working in a network is a major strand of government reform with much emphasis and funding being placed on collaborative support (Dering et al., 2006). In addition, as schools merge into multi-academy trusts (MATs) or Teaching School Alliances (TSAs), schools are increasingly working within a larger context or on a larger scale, increasing both the pressure on and the necessity for working in teams (Department for Education, 2019g). This can be viewed as a positive, with a caring work culture and inter-school collaboration supporting and therefore helping that teamwork and not hindering it (Marks et al., 2005; Pont et al., 2008). Organised networks play a critical role in supporting leaders in facing challenging circumstances, but these networks require continuous negotiation for them to work well (Dering et al., 2006). However, with increasing demands and accountability on schools and their teams to deliver results and the need for those teams to work increasingly effectively as a team, increased collaboration with others can positively affect that work (Ofsted, 2019b).

9.4 Team balance: communication and cooperation

Teams in schools function to ultimately improve the attainment and progress of the students and rely on 'conjoint processes and focused collaborative learning' (Harris and DeFlaminis, 2016, p. 143). As such, the commitment to collaboration in all cases includes a rejection of competitive individualism and personal achievement in favour of community goals, which are important to decision-making and team effectiveness (Hall and Wallace, 1996; McIntyre and Foti, 2013). This 'shared understanding of team goals, individual team member tasks, and the coordination of the team to achieve common goals' is referred to by McIntyre and Foti (2013, p. 47) as team mental models but does not include reference to the holistic, collective working as a team. Van Den Bossche et al.'s work (2006, p. 490), suggests that 'both interpersonal and socio-cognitive processes have to be taken into consideration' to understand collective teamwork. Their work recommends the study of both the behavioural and the socio-cognitive, including the ability of the team to interact, discuss, and negotiate.

Good internal communications and a developed team spirit based upon past successes makes a group much more likely to do well in its task area (Adair, 1973). Increased communication and increased connectivity help meet a need that has never been greater in working together effectively as part of a team. From their research, teams that were able to establish open communication and trust appeared to realise their potential as drivers of change (Dering et al., 2006; Sheard et al., 2009).

Top tip ...

Support and promote communication, collaboration, co-operation, and trust.

9.5 Team balance: team CPD

As teams are created and evolve, they tend to go through stages of maturity or development. Team development theory provides a conceptual framework for this process. Tuckman and Jensen's model (1977) of Forming (coming together as a new team), Storming (sorting out the differences between the team), Norming (moving to stability as a team), and Performing (everyone in the team achieving at or beyond expectations) has been the foundation on which most subsequent research has been developed (Kur, 1996; Rickards and Moger, 2000; Castka et al., 2003; Sheard et al., 2009). In addition, team learning is constructivist, relating to and building on previous experience, with self-directed change proving most effective, the team learning through social interaction and cooperation (Rogers, 1992; Honey and Mumford, 2000; Druskat and Pescosolido, 2002; Boyatzis, 2007).

This suggests that for the leader and the team, they should work collectively together and provide feedback to each other for the team's development to attain optimal effectiveness (Kolb, 1984; Sergiovanni, 2001; Wiyono, 2018). However, although a set of standards is in place for teachers through the Teachers' Standards (DfE, 2011) and for team leaders through the National Standards of Excellence for team leaders (DfE, 2020), there is an expectation for team leaders to develop themselves and distribute leadership through their team, albeit with no expectation to support or develop that team's leadership (Erich and Cranston, 2004).

With leadership development being a major strand of government reform and a body of research to inform and support team development, it is surprising how little of the government-supported leadership development is aimed at leadership team development (Dering et al., 2006). For example, although leaders through the National Professional Qualification for Middle Leaders (NPQML) are expected to 'support all members of their team' (DfE, 2021a, p. 16) and are assessed on this, there are no such expectations or assessment criteria for senior leaders undertaking the National Professional Qualification for Senior Leaders (NPQSL) nor for team leaders taking the National Professional Qualification for team leaders (NPQH) (DfE, 2019a; DfE, 2021a).

If this is representative, there is a need for both team development and team leader development in schools (Sheard et al., 2009). Given that such interventions are costly, growing capacity within the system through the development of consultancy and coaching skills may be critical to developing and ensuring team success (Dering et al., 2006). Thus, whereas there are qualifications and training opportunities available to help guide and develop team leaders, which would be a positive influence on their teams, there appears to be little, if any, guidance or development available for team leaders, which would be a negative influence on their work.

 Top tip ...

Provide CPD for team development as much as individual development

9.6 Team balance: school culture

The school culture can be a strong positive contributor to occupational wellbeing, according to Jerrim and Sims (2019). Everyone, from teaching assistants to senior leaders, in schools highly appreciates a strong sense of community at work, which can impact positively on their wellbeing. This sense of community arises from a strong sense of teamwork, a culture of collaboration and planning as a team, a supportive, no-blame culture, having shared values within a team, and a positive, inclusive, compassionate, and friendly ethos. Thus, school culture is an important external factor influencing teamwork in schools.

Charles Handy (2006) defines and classifies school culture in one of four ways:

- A power culture: a central power figure surrounded by ever widening circles of influence

- A role culture: a carefully and thoroughly organised bureaucracy

- A task culture: where groups or teams meet objectives/resolve issues

- A person culture that puts the individual first.

A key factor on effective teamwork is the level to which norms are accepted within an organisation that then sets the culture. The norms of a group help determine whether it functions as a highly effective team or not. A culture that is open, honest, and communicative, that honours difference and divergence, which embraces conflict and emotion and that fosters enquiry and reflection is more supportive of learning than one that is not. Conversely, when distrust pervades a school culture, it is unlikely that the school will be an energetic, motivating place (Mitchell and Sackney, 2000).

Schein (1984), Argyris (1985), and Mitchell and Sackney (2001) argue that organisational culture is a key factor in determining how far social learning is possible. For example, where lack of transparency and guarded relationships are the accepted norm within the group, then sharing is likely to be impaired. Therefore, the accepted norms within a school will affect the accepted norms within a team, with the team leader being the 'hinge pin within the team' (Moswela 2019, p. 448) that sets the acceptance or non-acceptance of those norms, which then sets the culture within a school (Goleman et al., 2002; Dering et al., 2006). To this end, culture is not primarily an external context but is an internal state of mind that underlies and influences the process of communication (Hall, 2002; Jameson, 2007; Levitt, 2014).

School-wide cultural norms: factors affecting the team	
Positive influences	**Negative influences**
Clear purpose	Unclear purpose
Consensual decisions	Unilateral decisions
Democratic	Hierarchical
Effectual working	Ineffectual working

Continued on next page

School-wide cultural norms: factors affecting the team

Positive influences	Negative influences
Communicative	Uncommunicative
Meaningful communication	Meaningless communication
Informality	Formality
Ability to listen	Inability to listen
Trust	Distrust
Openness	Closed
Honest	Dishonest
Embraces conflict	Rejects conflict
Embraces open conflict	Embraces private conflict
Fosters enquiry	Rejects enquiry
Fosters reflection	Rejects reflection
Evaluation of work is norm	Evaluation of work is rare

The table above draws together the positive or negative school-wide cultural norms (and therefore the positive or negative influences on a team) as identified by Mitchell and Sackney (2000), Dering et al. (2006), and Parker (2008). Such influences include action (e.g. 'reflection'), how well that action is done (e.g. 'effectual'), or express opposite ends of a continuum (e.g. 'trust – distrust').

Drawing these four bivariate factors together suggests a single important consideration: the prioritisation of the collective. This includes the setting and acceptance of collective norms, the training and development of the team, the distribution and shared understanding of what it means to be a team, and the ability to 'perform' and deliver as a team.

9.7 Team balance: definition ambiguity

With a plethora of theoretical frameworks (Northouse, 2016) and no mandatory national framework of expectations for team leaders from government (Hartle and Thomas, 2003; Dunford, 2016; DfE 2020; DfE 2021a), there is a lack of clarity for team leaders as to their expected role. What there is, comes either from government-funded schemes (e.g. Teach First or Future Leaders), or from the government's inspectorate, Ofsted, which frequently publishes its revised inspection framework for schools (Dunford, 2016; Ofsted, 2019a). The latter stipulates a number of expectations for the school leadership to achieve, including demonstrating 'ambitious vision', having 'high expectations' and ensuring 'high standards of provision' (Ofsted, 2019a, p. 74). However, this applies to the general leadership of the school, including governance, and does not provide a specific set of expectations for team leaders to follow. Thus, there appears to be no clear, specific criteria from government as to the expectations of a secondary team leader and what they should do

(Huber, 2004; Bush, 2008; DfE 2020; DfE 2021a). Furthermore, within the literature, the term 'team leader' and 'leader' are frequently interchanged, hence making the terms 'leader' (the team leader or senior leader) and 'leadership' (the action of the team leader, or senior leader, or senior leaders) unclear and complex (Grint, 2005; Shuffler, 2013; Kerns, 2019).

To compound this, most researchers align with the view that the term 'leadership' is also a process of influencing in which an individual exerts intentional influence over others to structure activities and relationships in a group or organisation (Yukl, 2013; Buble et al., 2014) with Bush and Glover (2003) including leadership being exercised by teams as well as individuals. Consequently, there appears to be no clear definition of leadership (Huber, 2004; Bush, 2008), and this therefore renders the term teamwork open to (mis)interpretation. As a result, although having a clear internal definition of their individual role may have a positive influence on the individual school leader, the external interchangeability of leadership terms and subsequent misinterpretations and misunderstandings may have a negative influence on the team.

9.8 Team balance: team ethos

Fundamental to the effective working of any team, is a set of shared values and beliefs, as illustrated by Westerbeek and Smith's (2005) team leadership pyramid below. The pyramid below illustrates what needs to be in place for effective team performance. On the journey of the leadership team to lead staff and engender a greater consensus with them to successfully achieve the school's goals (two arrows), the leader must first identify, agree, and utilise a set of common values or norms within the school community (base layer of the pyramid). Once these are established, goals and objectives are set so that the direction of travel is clear and any support that is needed is offered. This all helps develop a motivated workforce, feeling pride and satisfaction in the accomplishments achieved together, finally acknowledging the team's work and success.

Figure 9.1 Westerbeek and Smith's hierarchy of team needs (2005)

Because this team pyramid is founded on common (mutually agreed) values and beliefs, this is a positive or negative influence on the team's work because some of those values or beliefs may be positive, such as trust, or negative, such as mistrust.

As well as the shared values and beliefs the team may have, how they come to make decisions may also be viewed as a positive or negative, depending on how they are handled. Decision theory, as developed by MacCrimmon (1968) and popularised by Myerson (1991), has two branches: descriptive decision theory (how decisions are made) and normative decision theory (what decisions are optimal given the circumstances).

These theories propose that for the leader and the team, the process of how decisions are made should be clear, so that the decisions made are the best and most effective for each circumstance (Vroom and Yetton, 1973; Vroom and Jago, 1988; Edmondson et al., 2002). In relation to personal norms, the most significant follow normative decision theory and include the effort to achieve the set goals and commitment to the team's success. Similarly, in relation to group norms, the most significant also follow normative decision theory and include communication, cooperation, potency, and cohesion, with the work of the group being coordinated by the team leader (Harangus and Duda-Daianu, 2011; Allan, 2019; Moswela, 2019; Wiyono, 2019). A critical fault with many team leaders in decision-making is to suppress the individual in favour of the many (Westerbeek and Smith, 2005). To help overcome these difficulties, Eraut (1994) emphasised the importance of creating the 'social space' for meaningful interaction to occur.

There are implications here, regarding social space, with how time is structured within the working week and how opportunities for productive dialogue between the team are created within schools at each stage of the process (Dering et al., 2006). However, critics of teamwork (Sennett, 1998; Sinclair, 1992) suggest it is superficially demeaning and a form of ideological tyranny (Hall, 2002). Sinclair suggests the need to analyse teams in terms of the degree of coercion, not cohesion, within the team; the concealment of conflict under the guise of consensus; conformity stemming creativity; the pretence of corporate decision-making; delayed action through consultation; and the obfuscation of expedient arguments and personal agendas (Sinclair, 1992).

Micropolitics

In their research, Ehrich and Cranston (2004) suggested that when members of a team become involved in power play, coercion, duplicity, cooperation, co-option, and influence, there is a more political agenda to their work and as such has a negative influence on the effective working of the team (Hall and Wallace, 1996; Bush et al., 2012). This may be especially true for the team leader, who may misuse or even abuse their power and influence on the team in a negative way (Benoliel, 2017).

However, where micropolitics works well, it provides a useful conceptual framework to understand the internal interactions of the team and can enable the team to be more effectively cooperative and facilitative with each other (Cranston and Ehrich, 2009).

This final factor highlights the importance of the team's internal norms; how they are set, agreed, discussed, and amended. In addition, how they make the best decisions for the school.

 Top tip ...

Be clear about what the 'real' accepted behaviours are in the team and in the school and where they need changing – change them.

9.9 Team balance: clear goals

While the quality of teaching is the most important factor in improving pupil progress, it is perhaps the quality of leadership and management that is the most important factor on school effectiveness and improvement (Huber, 2004; Scheerens, 2012; Miller, 2016). Almost every study of school effectiveness has shown leadership, as a process of interactive events that occur in groups, to be a key factor (Sammons et al., 1995). Therefore, understanding teams is intrinsic to understanding leadership. Leadership is thus about managing the functions that are important to the group and securing the accomplishment of its goals (Daniels et al., 2019). As a result, leaders who gain the credibility of their staff and peers are regarded as effective. Within the context of a school, the goal of education is to ensure that teaching and learning takes place successfully and the students achieve (Kozlowski et al., 2009; Sheard et al., 2009; Kogler-Hill, 2016; Moswela, 2019). Hence, for the team to be viewed as and to be effective, having clear goals and achieving them is a factor that has a positive influence on team teamwork. In consequence, this ensures that the work to be completed by the team is kept only to the work that is necessary to achieve the school's goals and regarded as their optimal workload.

 Top tip ...

Have clear goals, a clear task structure with clear process and procedures for everyone to follow to ensure team success.

9.10 Team balance: the internet

The ability for teams to communicate and work together as a team, in ways other than being in one room together at the same time, through their use of ICT, has revolutionised both the teamwork of businesses and school teamwork in schools (Kozlowski et al., 2009).

The ability to communicate and work together as a team has never been greater (Raja, 2018). Following the COVID-19 pandemic, the educational world has seen a change in how it uses technology (Shenoy et al., 2020; Varela and Fedynich, 2020), shifting with dramatic speed from the management and leadership of e-learning (Jameson, 2015) to e-leadership. This is experienced by school-based teams via the ability to email or text groups, to edit documents or policies concurrently via such programmes as Google Docs or Dropbox, and the ability to conference call from different locations through such products as Microsoft Teams, Skype Business, Zoom, or Google Meet. All these enable teamwork to take place concurrently but not necessarily in the same location (Raja, 2018). Thus, previous restrictions, such as travel time and arranging meeting space, have been reduced or removed, creating more time for the team and allowing them to function as a team more effectively (Thompson, 2003; Dube and Robey, 2009; Heng-Yu, 2013), with increased engagement and attendance (Shenoy et al., 2020). Other advantages include more focused discussion, higher-quality contributions, more participation, and increased flexibility of working (Qiu and McDougall, 2013). Disadvantages include a heavier workload through the addition of using technology (e.g. the need to print out documents), time delays, and loss of train of thought; and cold messaging and misunderstanding the meaning or inference in a communication (ibid.).

In summarising the external factors having a positive influence, the literature suggests that there needs to be clarity, that is, clear goals or clear structures, for the team to work as effectively as possible. Also, support to help the work of the team be more effective can come from external sources such as technology or other education establishments.

 Top tip ...

Use the internet as much as possible – it has significant pros (and significant cons).

9.11 Team balance: team leadership

Leading the team effectively and managing the work of the team flexibly is critical to the success of the team (Barnett and McCormick, 2012).

To manage the increased pressure and meet the higher demands placed on them by government, it is widely accepted by researchers that teams are embedded in the everyday life of leading schools (Kozlowski et al., 2009). There are two distinctly different interpretations on leadership, the born-to-lead school, and the self-development school (Sheard et al., 2009). The born-to-lead school, whereby the leader is a master of themselves and others, follows Nietzsche's 'Übermensch' model, while the Socratic 'What ought one to do?' model combines intellect with learning and humility, the leader being a catalyst for questioning and finding answers. Both led to styles of leadership in the 1990s, such as transformational, charismatic, and visionary leadership, but which were all centred on the individual (Gronn, 2002).

Distributed leadership, though having its roots in the 1950s, emerged more robustly in the 1990s due to the need to divide increased labour to the team and was put into play because of a disillusionment with exceptional leaders who were proved to be unrealistic and unsustainable (Hall and Wallace, 1996; Gronn, 2002; Barnett and McCormick, 2012).

It was a fashionable new imperative coinciding with a shift in research from psychologists studying small interpersonal groups to the study of work teams (Timperley, 2005; Westerbeek and Smith, 2005; Kozlowski et al., 2009; O'Donoghue and Clarke, 2010).

Early proponents of distributed leadership recognised that leadership could be shared with and through others (Adair, 1973) and be either additive (dispersed or delegated to the individuals in a group) or holistic (to the collective team) (Gibb, 1968; Gronn, 2002). O'Donoghue and Clarke (2010) saw it as 'integral to achieving the outcome' (the promotion of learning), as leadership CPD programmes highlighted the innate leadership capacity of the whole team, not just the team leader, to influence the promotion of learning, not just the principal, making a positive difference to the leadership of a school (Supovitz and Riggan, 2012).

Distributed leadership is therefore the distribution of leadership practice rather than distributing roles or distributing responsibilities (Harris and DeFlaminis, 2016) and continues to have an influence within educational policy. This is still the case in England today with the government making it explicit that leadership practice through expecting team leaders to provide 'successful leadership and management of teams and individuals within their schools' (DfE, 2020).

In moving from the singular leadership of the team leader to the distributed leadership of the team which is shared amongst the team, creates a sharper focus on the interactions between the team (Daniels, 2019). This mode of managing the increased external demands and expectations on leadership in schools has made distributed leadership the prevalent mode of school leadership in the past 40 years (Marks et al., 2005). However, within the literature, there appears to be no clear definition of distributed leadership (Harris, 2013). As a result, while distributed leadership may be a positive influence on the team, the lack of definition of it is likely to be a negative influence on the understanding and practice of it. Therefore, although the status of school teams has remained the same, the workload of these teams has significantly increased, which is a combination of both positive (increased responsibility) and negative (increased workload) influences on the team's work. None of this is helped by 'the absence of a neat and consistent definition of distributed leadership' (Harris and DeFlaminis, 2016, p. 141).

For team leaders to make lone decisions is irrational (Harangus and Duda-Daianu, 2011). Leadership requires the team leader to know themselves and their teams, to develop them and support their decision-making (Sheard et al., 2009). It is thus important for a group leader to understand how their group is developing into a credible, performing team and ensure this happens (Miller, 2016; DfE, 2021a).

While outstanding teams make certain they receive more information, higher rewards, and more development, and struggling teams remain insufficiently considered and under-resourced, there will be an effect on school improvement (Wageman et al., 2008). Hence, the facilitation and development of effective teamwork is an essential and not a luxury, and research recommends that team leaders think twice about neglecting their support for and the development of their team (Dering et al., 2006).

For the individual new to a team, a difficult period of mutual adjustment usually follows the commencement of a new role, where the new team member must work hard to gain the acceptance of others (Hall and Wallace, 1996; Westerbeek and Smith, 2005). It is therefore essential that there is a carefully planned induction into the team as well as the school (Dunham, 1995).

For the team, several team development models exist, which include Tuckman's model of team development (1977), the Myers Briggs Type Indicator tool (1978), Honey and Mumford's Learning Styles (2000), and Belbin's team dynamics (2010). However, these are development tools geared to an individual within a team rather than to the individuals as a collective team (Allan, 2019). Tuckman's model appears to be the only team development model available to teams and is an area that is under-researched (Kozlowski et al., 2009). Consequently, a positive or negative influence on a team's effective work is in how well the team leader knows the team, how well the team is developing, and how effectively the team leader is managing that development.

Leader centrism

Several researchers have indicated that team leadership is central to team processes, with the impetus to work with and through a team coming initially from the team leader (Parker, 2008; Belbin, 2010; Barnett and McCormick, 2016). This approach can only operate if the team leader advocates it, though their advocacy does not ensure success, despite the team leader's considerable power to shape the culture of the teamwork that emerges (Hall and Wallace, 1996).

While the leadership of the team leader is critically important to an organization (Adair, 1973; Sammons et al., 1995; Dering et al., 2006), the team leader has an ambiguous role in the team, especially a team leader, having to be both leader and sometimes follower, representing hierarchy through their formal position and encouraging equality of contribution through their teamwork, in a role that is now both more important and more difficult than it has ever been (Parker, 2008). The strength of a team's work depends not only on the team leader's capacity to move between these positions but also on the other team members' willingness to do the same.

The role of the team leader, thus, holds special sway concerning emotional intelligence effectiveness (Goleman et al., 2002; Day and Sammons, 2013). The interactions between the team are coordinated in such a way as to secure the most efficient and effective way of working and it is the group leader who sets the tone and helps create the groups' emotional reality (Dunham, 1995) as identified by Goleman (1992).

	Commanding	Visionary	Affiliative	Democratic	Pacesetting	Coaching
The leader's approach	Demand immediate compliance from the team	Mobilise the team toward a vision	Creates harmony/builds bonds within the team	Forges consensus/participation from the team	Sets high standards of performance by the team	Develops the team for the future
The style in a phrase	'Do what I tell you'	'Come with me'	'The team/others come first'	'What do you think'	'Do as I do now'	'Try this'
Underlying emotional intelligence competencies	Drive to achieve, initiative, self-control	Self-confidence, empathy, change catalyst	Empathy, building relationships, communication	Collaboration, team leadership, communication	Conscientiousness, drive to achieve, initiative	Developing others, empathy, self-awareness
When this style works best	In a crisis	When changes require a new vision	To heal rifts in the team	To build buy-in or consensus	To get quick results	To help the team improve performance
Overall impact on the team	Negative	Most strongly positive	Positive	Positive	Negative	Positive

Strong leaders know how to keep the balance between accomplishing the tasks in hand and maintaining harmonious relationships among the team, and a leader who is not emotionally intelligent can wreak havoc in a team situation (Goleman et al., 2002). Indeed there is a clear link between leadership styles and the motivation on the team (Buble et al., 2014).

In their work, they found that

a soft authoritarian leadership style with significant elements of consultative leadership style, dominates in this sample, especially at the higher levels of management, as opposed to the lower levels, where an almost pure authoritarian style of leadership dominates. These results, regardless of the fact that Croatian society is a conservative society, are certainly not encouraging, bearing in mind today's business trends that require.

(p. 189)

Therefore, the ability of the team leader to successfully be a team player (as an equal), the team captain (as an expert) and where relevant, the team manager (as the employer) when inside the team is critical to the team's success. Thus, this role has a different dynamic to the others within the team (Wageman et al., 2008; Barnett and McCormick, 2012). The role of the head of department or team leader in a team creates a trichotomy for the team in their collective interaction: whether the head of department or team leader is engaging in the work of the team as a team player (equal), the team leader (expert), or in the case of the team leader, the team manager (employer). Reframing the ego is just one of the many development tasks that those involved in teamwork must undertake (Hall, 2002). Consequently, for teamwork to be effective, both the team leader and the team need to be clear as to their roles in any team decision-making. This is known as leader centrism.

Researchers have taken different positions in how leader centrism functions in that either the leader determines their followers (Kelley, 1988), there is an interchangeability between leaders and followers (Yukl, 2013), or that the followers determine their leader (Meindl, 1995). However, it is the situation that determines to what extent a decision can be shared. Sharing ever-expanding and complex demands with other leaders in an increasing age of accountability is high risk for the team leader and, in the absence of information, advice, and guidance from research as to the best methodology to lead a team, the team leader is unlikely to adopt another leadership style different from those with which the team are already comfortable (Hall and Wallace, 1996; Hall, 2002). This may be to the detriment of the leadership of the team. Other limiting factors may be in the personality of the leader, or the culture of an organisation (Adair, 1973; Yang et al., 2010).

Researchers have suggested the team leader should lead the team in different ways, depending on the requirements of the situation. Parker (2008) presents a framework that describes different leadership styles employed by team leaders to lead their team, including that of Contributor (feeding information to the team), Collaborator (bringing in contributions from all the team), Communicator (articulating the views of the team), and Challenger (challenging the views of the team).

Belbin (2010) suggests that the team leader as Chairman (coordinator or shaper) should be trusting by nature, have strong basic dominance, have a strong and morally based commitment to external goals and objectives, be calm and unflappable, be a practical realist, have basic self-discipline, and be detached and distant in social situations. Others are less specific, suggesting that the team leader sets the team's direction, manages its operations, and develops its self-management capacity (Barnett and McCormick, 2016; Moswela, 2019).

A key issue that arises here is team accountability. If the team are able and have the capacity to hold themselves to account, then a flatter, more democratic model of power distribution can be in place. If, for whatever reason, the team are not able, or do not have the capacity to hold themselves to account, then a steeper, more hierarchical model of power distribution must be in place (Hall, 2002). Thus, the team leader as team manager, leader, and player, together with the team, must be responsive to the situational needs and manage the situation accordingly. This requires them all to adjust their leadership style to the situation and be adaptable. Being able to do this is a key factor of high motivation and productivity (Kozlowski et al., 2009; O'Donoghue and Clarke, 2010; Buble et al., 2014) and may be a positive or a negative influence on the team's effective working, dependent on how well the team leader and the team manage it.

Team plurality

Teamwork is a multi-dimensional construct, working within an organisation, having a collective identity, and constituting multiple individuals (Adair, 1983). For the leader and the team, therefore, they should always be aware of and consider the multi-dimensional nature of their work for it to attain optimal effectiveness (Stott and Walker, 1995; Castka et al., 2003). The team should always be aware of and consider the resultant convergence and divergence of agreement within the team and manage the work of the team accordingly for it to attain optimal effectiveness (Stewart and Manz, 1995; Marks et al., 2000; Kozlowski et al., 2009; McIntyre and Foti, 2013).

The effective management of staff requires the team leader to view as equally important, the task, the team, and the individuals within the team (Adair, 1973; Dunham, 1995). Adair recommends that five key stage actions be completed to successfully achieve the management objectives. These are defining team objectives (involving the team and gaining shared commitment), planning (consult, encourage ideas, and suggestions), brief the team (answer questions and gain feedback), support and monitor the team (coordinate the team and resolve any conflict), and evaluate the team's work (recognise success, learn from failure).

This indicates that the management of the team should be proportionately balanced between the individual, the team, and the tasks of the team, but this will depend on how the team is managed and how open the team is to be managed. Hall and Wallace (1996) considered that the internal process of teamwork 'was judged to be successful according to the strength of individual contributions and the quality of the decisions made' (Hall and Wallace, 1996, p. 304). Both depend, in turn, on the way in which the team was 'managed' by both the team leader and the team members (Hall and Wallace, 1996). Kickul and Neuman later concurred that 'leaders play an integral part in modelling the team and setting the priorities for the team to successfully engage within it' (Kickul and Neuman, 2000 p. 27). Hence, a factor that could positively or negatively influence the effective teamwork of the team is, again, the ability of the team leader and the team to successfully manage themselves.

 Top tip

Empower and motivate others through meaningful distributed leadership

9.12 Team balance: team performance

There is overwhelming agreement that professional learning, although not a magic bullet, is directly and persistently linked to educational improvement (Mitchell and Sackney, 2000). Educational improvement may be achieved in two ways; the result justifying the means, or the means justifying the result. For a 'learning organisation' (ibid. p. 6), the end results are of the utmost importance, giving credibility to organisational growth, productivity, efficiency, and effectiveness. The means are the people and the learning taking place within the school. On the other hand, what is of importance to a 'learning community' (ibid., p. 6) are how the results are produced; the growth, development and learning of the people. For the learning community, it is how the community work and learn together that are important (ibid.).

Traditionally, schools have been learning communities, focusing on the learning process, rather than being a learning organisation focusing on results (Mitchell and Sackney, 2000). However, for a school to be effective, it must provide its pupils with both academic (results) and social experiences (confidence) to be a success (Sammons et al., 1995).

As schools are being increasingly defined by their results and outcomes (Harpham, 2020), with the need for teachers and leaders to show less transparency and more opacity (Ball, 2003), in this age of performativity, the goal, whether academic or social, is increasingly the end, not the means to that end, and schools can progressively be regarded as educational organisations to produce results (the product of learning) rather than an educational community to deliver learning (the process of learning) (Hall, 2002; Dunford, 2016), leaving learning to be open to misinterpretation (Ball, 2003). Hence, the debate between the government, which may see the need for education to be rebalanced in favour of results, and the teaching profession, which sees the process of learning being challenged, will continue unabated (Dunford, 2016; Harpham, 2020).

In summary, both these external factors have a single root: the government's need to evidence progress (Ball, 2008). Through an increased emphasis on results over people (Harpham, 2020) and increased data management in schools, these factors may both have a negative influence on the team, through increased staff turnover, lower morale, and increased workload (Dunford, 2016).

The national context that affects all schools in England includes the fluctuating statutory requirements on education as stipulated by the government (DfE, 2011a) and the auditing of these expectations of sound practice by inspectorates such as Ofsted (2019a) and more locally by education authorities. Thus, there are significant external factors on the work of school teams that are out of their control that both positively 'invite and incite us to make ourselves more effective' (Ball, 2008, p. 50), and at the same time negatively influence teamwork through creating 'ontological insecurity' and 'deprofessionalisation' (ibid., p. 55). A further external factor to influence the team is the culture of the school and the external accountability and expectations imposed on the team by the school (Riaz and Sultan, 2017). This creates a working environment where, like politicians, school teams are judged on their actions as much as their words. This section explores those factors in more detail.

According to Cannon (2016), education has always been subservient to politics and any attempt to extricate education from politics would be futile. History, it seems, would agree. The pace of change in education legislation of at least a law a year since the 1980s, compared to only nine education acts in the previous 75 years, clearly demonstrates this increasing subservience (Wright, 2005; Gillard, 2018). Furthermore, since 1979, with subsequent governments continuing the trend of holding schools to account with what has become known as 'performativity', school teams are under pressure to 'perform' (Ball, 2008; Harpham, 2020), especially in English Language, Maths, and Science (DfE, 2019c). This pressure is felt by all schools through quinquennial Section 5 inspections from Ofsted; inspections within 30 months if the school is deemed to 'Require Improvement' or to be 'Inadequate'; or through the annual publication of their GCSE and A level results introduced in 2016 (Ofsted, 2019a; DfE, 2019c). Pressure from government and the pace of statutory and regulatory change is increasing and is more mobile and more volatile than it has ever been (Dunford, 2016; Gillard, 2018; Harpham, 2020). In addition, the need to both 'report on what we do as well as doing it' (Ball, 2008, p. 57), increases the workload of teams on schools.

Moreover, with the DfE reporting that schools in England have improved in the past decade, from 66% of schools being judged as 'Good' or 'Outstanding' in 2010 to 85% in 2018 (DfE, 2019d; DfE, 2019h), this justifies their strategy and suggests the pressure on teams is unlikely to dissipate in the immediate future.

This is supported by recent results on the international stage, according to the Programme for International Student Assessment (PISA), where student achievement in England, particularly in Mathematics, has significantly improved in the last three years (DfE, 2019b). This provides a further justification for the government to continue its drive for school improvement and counters the views of researchers, such as Dimmock (2000) and MacBeath (2007), who encourage a greater focus on teaching and learning lessons in schools and a return to 'real' education, rather than always preparing for tests (O'Donoghue and Clarke, 2010).

While Wallace observed a decade in the 1990s where school leaders had lost their freedom to be visionaries due to government reforms (Wallace, 2001), Smyth (2006) argued that conditions in schools were deteriorating through increased emphasis on accountability, standards, measurement, and high stakes testing, for the benefit of key stakeholders; for example, parents, the government, or Ofsted (O'Donoghue and Clarke, 2010; DfE, 2019b). These sources support the view that the drive for improved outcomes in recent years has succeeded. Indeed, in their research, Solomon and Lewin (2016) concluded that:

> while these (pedagogical) innovations were considered to be of major benefit to both teachers and pupils, a fundamental contradiction between the focus on individual development underpinning the new approach and the demands of accountability in a persistent culture of performativity proved to be insurmountable.
>
> (Solomon and Lewin, 2016, p. 226)

Thus, this increased pressure from government is a combination of both positive (securing improved results for the students) and negative (creates new demands, increasing workload) influences on school teamwork.

Top tip ...

Focus on learning (i.e. school improvement), not data and 'performing'.

9.13 Team balance: processes and procedures

A further aspect to teamwork, viewed by the research as positive, is in well-managed team processes. When team processes are aligned with task demands, the team is effective; when they are not, the team is ineffective (Sheard et al., 2009).

Team effectiveness is consequently based on the concept inherent in the research over the last 40 years of input–process–output. In this framework the input refers to the characteristics and qualities of the group or team; the process is the interaction of that team with the task they need to accomplish; the output is the collective action of the team in completing (or not) the task requirements (Daniels et al., 2019).

The initiative to create or change a team to meet that goal comes more effectively from the team leader and therefore, by definition, is hierarchical in genesis. Moving from teamwork (multiple, disconnected working) to teamwork (collective, connected working) is about creating conditions for group effectiveness and is an evolutionary process (Hall, 2002). Thus, it is the responsibility of the team leader to regularly monitor and maintain the effectiveness of the team and ensure it is being sufficiently supported and developed (Hall, 2002; Kozlowski, 2009). As team processes are more closely linked to team effectiveness than tasks, teams and team leaders are more likely to be effective more quickly by focusing attention and improvement on their internal processes than on the tasks they perform (Hall, 2002). Hence, teamwork theory proposes, for the leader and the team, prioritising a focus on improving team processes to more quickly attain optimal effectiveness and deliver increased job satisfaction (Klimoski and Mohammed, 1994; Druskat and Pescosolido, 2002; Mierlo et al., 2005; Rasmussen, 2006) and so is a positive factor on the team's work.

Drawing this section together, it identifies the importance of the team's make-up and internal interactions. This includes having shared communication, collaboration, trust, and an understanding of what it means to be part of a team. It also identifies the importance of having balanced and well-managed processes and procedures within the team.

9.14 Team balance: clear tasks

Another important factor in effective teamwork is in the team construction and composition, offering a sense of belonging and membership, with structures; for example, a team hierarchy or systems of accountability and boundaries that frame the team (Kogler-Hill, 2016).

However, if the group lacks structure, decision-making quality and speed suffer. Equally, where the team do not work well together, they create barriers and disharmony across the school (Dunham, 1995; Goleman et al., 2002; Kozlowski et al., 2009). Indeed, the type of task performed by the team affects productivity and satisfaction; the more complex the task, the higher the level of satisfaction. Kent and McGrath in the 1960s found that 80% of the variance in a group's performance (effectiveness) was due to the characteristics of the task, rather than the characteristics of the group (Currall et al., 2001). This challenges Belbin's (2010) view that it is the characteristics of the group that determine the success or otherwise of the group and supports the view that getting the task structure right enables the team to be more effective. Since people are responsible for completing their tasks successfully, within a team, both points are valid. Within a team, it is the effective combination of people that helps promote team success. However, it is also effectively matching the tasks that need to be done with the best people in the team to accomplish them that also determines the success of the team. Again, having a clear task structure ensures that the work to be completed by the team is kept only to the work that is necessary to achieve the school's goals (optimal workload).

Top tip ...

Have clear goals, a clear task structure with clear process and procedures for everyone to follow to ensure team success.

9.15 Team balance: trust

Trust is a critical factor in bringing profound improvement to a school. Without trust, people divert their energy into self-protection and away from learning. Where trust is lacking, people will not take the risks necessary to move the school forward. Without trust, communication tends to be distorted, making it more difficult to solve problems (Mitchell and Sackney, 2000). When distrust pervades a school culture, it is unlikely that the school will be an energetic, motivating place.

Trust is thus an element of social capital (Kickul and Neuman, 2000). Unsuccessful teams are a product of the workplace culture; the faults of the management team epitomise the faults of the firm that they lead (Belbin, 2010). Hence, intrinsic factors that may affect the effective working of a team are the individual's choice to cooperate, collaborate, and trust (internal socio-cognitive), and then act accordingly as a team (external behaviours) (Van Den Bossche, 2006; Belbin, 2010; Moswela, 2019).

Therefore, cooperation, collaboration, and trust are integral positive factors on the effective work of the team. This can be enhanced by the team leader, who can build an effective climate for teamwork through valuing the contributions of colleagues (affirmation) and inviting them to be participants (invitation) (Mitchell and Sackney, 2000). Conversely, reluctant or subversive team players can undermine the effective working of the team, through being uncooperative, uncollaborative, and distrustful (Hall and Wallace, 1996; Wallace, 2001; McIntyre and Foti, 2013).

9.16 Team balance: vision and values

A shared vision or mental model as a theoretical representation of teamwork (see an example of an organisational line management structure below) are 'precursors to effective team performance and make a positive difference' (McIntyre and Foti, 2013, p. 48). This suggests that for the leader and the team, they should have a clear, frequently shared theoretical understanding of their work as a team. This way, it is a positive factor on the team's work as it will help the team to more quickly attain optimal effectiveness (Mathieu et al., 2000; Druskat and Pescosolido, 2002; Senior and Swailes, 2007; Salas et al., 2009).

9.17 Team balance: workload

Secondary school leaders are working approximately 57 hours a week, a decrease of just under 6 hours a week compared to 2013 (Ofsted, 2019c; DfE, 2019e). Team leaders are reported to work approximately 62 hours a week, with 43% of them indicating that their workload is unmanageable, representing an increase of 36% since 2013 (Jerrim and Sims, 2019). Also, these figures are significantly higher than the 1,265 hours (32.4 hours per week) expected, as detailed in the School Teachers' Pay and Conditions (DfE, 2019e; DfE, 2019f; Ofsted, 2019c). This is effectively illustrated in Blake and Mouton's grid below, which maps out the concern for people or for results from low (1) to high (9) concern.

Up until the 1980s, schools were left to lead themselves with little government control (Gillard, 2018); concern for people was higher and an emphasis on results, lower (red box, 'past' on the grid below. However, a shift in school culture occurred after the introduction of the Education Reform Act (1988), which increased the power culture in schools, located in the role of the team leader and subsequently distributed to other leaders and their teams. This also increased the role culture (increased organisational responsibilities), while maintaining a task culture (the personnel remaining the same) and diminishing the people culture (putting people second).

This indicates the shift from 'past' (6/6) to 'present' (5/7) as illustrated below (Dunham, 1995, with my additions). Moreover, there has been an increase in the number of MATs (a chain of schools with an overarching 'lead school', n = 1,170, introduced in 2014), TSAs (an alliance of schools supported by an 'Outstanding' school, n = 650, introduced in 2011) and National Leaders of Education (team leaders of 'Outstanding' schools supporting other schools, n = 1182, introduced in 2014) – none of which existed pre-2011. These groupings add to the responsibilities and workload of the team leader and therefore adds to the responsibilities and workload of their team (DfE, 2019g). This emphasises the increasing influence (power culture) of the team leader and increases the workload (role culture), without necessarily increasing the size of the team.

	1/1	2	3	4	5	6	7	8	9/1
High	1/9								9/9
	8							Ideal	
	7								
Concern	6					Past			
for	5				5/5		Present		
people	4								
	3								
	2								
Low	1/1	2	3	4	5	6	7	8	9/1
Low				Concern for results					High

It appears that in the drive for improved results, there has been less of a concern by government for people (high working hours over a sustained period) coupled with a large focus on task completion. While closer to the 'ideal' (8/8) of high concern for both people and results, this appears to have less concern for people, higher concern for task completion and an increased workload (Solomon and Lewin, 2016; Jerrim and Sims, 2019). Because teams are best placed to meet increasing demands and challenges from government (Currall et al., 2001), the ability to work effectively as a team has never been of more importance. There is a need for teams in schools to be delivering in the long term, sharing the workload, and learning from each other (Sheard et al., 2009). Teamwork improves the decision-making and the quality assurance of the team's work. Hence, with sustained high(er) expectations for increased results from government comes the increased need for leadership to be delegated or distributed, with a balance of concern for people and results (Solomon and Lewin, 2016).

Wallace (2001) suggests that, within a school culture, there are incompatibilities in being both hierarchical (through structures, responsibilities or pay) and democratic (through decision-making or consultation). However, Katzenbach and Smith's research (1993) claims that hierarchy and teamwork are neither incompatible nor mutually exclusive. I would agree with Katzenbach and Smith and argue that such structures are not incompatible where such organisations require differing structures for them to function effectively. What is needed in such organisations is for those involved to be sufficiently pragmatic and adaptable to make such different structures work.

Top tip ...

Manage your workload and the micropolitics within the team.

9.18 Summary

Factor	Source	Average influence size	Detail /17.5	Average influence	Detail
School factor	Students	Large	14.5	Positive/ Negative	+31.5/ −29
External factor	Government	Large	14.5	Negative	−42.5/+5.5
Team Factor	Expertise	Large	14	Positive/ Negative	+34/−16.5
School factor	Staff	Large	14	Negative/ Positive	−48.5/ + 29.5
Team norm	Communication	Moderately large	13	Positive/ Negative	+57.5/−21.5
Team factor	Leadership	Moderately large	13	Positive	+38.5/−12
Team norm	Cohesion	Moderately large	13	Positive	+37/-2
School norm	Support	Moderately large	13	Positive	+30.5/−4.5
School norm	Ethos	Moderately large	12.5	Positive	+34/-7
School norm	Expectations	Moderately large	12.5	Positive/ Negative	+22.5/−19.5
External factor	COVID-19	Moderately large	11	Negative/ Positive	-36.5/+15.5
Team factor	Roles	Moderately large	10.5	Positive/ Negative	+32/−−15.5
School factor	Workload	Moderately large	10.5	Negative	-29.5/+6.5
External factor	Funding	Moderately large	10	Negative	-31/+3.5
Team factor	Delivery	Moderately small	9.5	Positive/ Negative	+19.5/−15.5
School factor	Parents	Moderately small	9	Negative/ Positive	+8.5/−19
Team Norm	Meetings	Moderately small	8.5	Positive	+27/-6

Continued on next page

Factor	Source	Average influence size	Detail /17.5	Average influence	Detail
Team factor	Personalities	Moderately small	8.5	Positive/ Negative	+22.5/−8.5
Team norm	Decision-making	Moderately small	8.5	Positive/ Negative	+17.5/−12
Team norm	Openness	Moderately small	8	Positive	+20.5/0
External factor	Ofsted	Moderately small	8	Negative/ Positive	−17.5/+15
School norm	Accountability	Moderately small	8	Negative/ Positive	−17.5/+13.5
Team norm	Collaboration	Moderately small	7.5	Positive	+10/−0.5
School factor	Governors	Moderately small	7.5	Positive/ Negative	+12.5/−7.5
School Norm	Subversion	Moderately small	6.5	Negative	−20.5/+0.5
School factor	Legacy	Moderately small	6.5	Negative	−29/+9.5
School norm	Teaching	Moderately small	6	Positive	+9/−2
School factor	Vision	Moderately small	6.5	Positive/ Negative	+22/−12.5
Team factor	Trust	Moderately small	5.5	Positive	+12/−1
School norm	Innovation	Moderately small	5.5	Positive	+9.5/−2.5
School factor	Structures	Moderately small	5	Positive/ Negative	+10/−7.5
School norm	Duties	Moderately small	5	Positive/ Negative	+7/−6.5
External factor	School Roll	Moderately small	5	Negative	−7.5/+1
School norm	Professionalism	Moderately small	5	Positive	+12.5/−0.5
Team norm	Targets	Small	4.5	Positive/ Negative	+6.5/−5.5
School norm	Respect	Small	4	Positive	+7/0
School norm	CPD	Small	3.5	Positive	+7.5/−1

Continued on next page

Factor	Source	Average influence size	Detail /17.5	Average influence	Detail
External factor	Industry	Small	3.5	Positive/ Negative	+6/−4
School factor	Safeguarding	Small	3.5	Negative/ Positive	+3/−5.5
School norm	Consultation	Small	3	Positive/ Negative	+10/−3.5
School factor	Middle leaders	Small	2.5	Negative/ Positive	+1.5/−4.5
External factor	Performance	Small	2.5	Negative/ Positive	−6.5/+3
External factor	Competition	Small	2.5	Negative	−14/+2
External factor	LEA	Small	2	Negative	−2.5/+0.5
Team norm	Emergency	Small	0.5	Negative/ Positive	+0.5 /−1

10 Concluding thoughts

Concluding this particular journey, I hope you are clearer as to the importance in teamwork of the need for clear expectations of the team; strong, collective actions and behaviours by the team; positive relationships between the team; a functional infrastructure to support the team; and an effective team training programme to develop the team.

I hope you are also clearer about the ability to ascertain within the team of which you are a part, or which you lead, the extent to which these ingredients are present, are present and doing what they need to do, or are present and doing what they need to do sufficiently well.

 **Top tip ...**

Team starting point: ascertain to what extent these ingredients are present, are present and doing what they need to do, or are present and doing what they need to do sufficiently well.

My journey in writing this book started with the presentation of the idea at an interview in a non-descript room in a campus of Greenwich University. It is the foresight and ability to see the potential in that idea by Professor Ade-Ojo that enabled me and complete the research into it. This academic part of the journey ends this term with my doctoral graduation.

My authorial journey in writing this book continues on from my two earlier books, *Progress Plain and Simple* and *The School Leader's Year*. The foresight and ability to see the potential in this idea as a book by Routledge editor Annamarie Kino enabled me to write this book. The fact that you are reading this now indicates that this particular authorial part of the journey is complete.

 DOI: 10.4324/9781003303404-10

And so, dear reader, it is now over to you and your own teamwork journey. It is over to you to complete your team audits and:

▓ Identify which part of teamwork is missing and add it

▓ Identify which part of teamwork needs improving and improve it

▓ Identify what standard of teamwork is required and reach it.

As John Donne observed over 400 years ago, 'No man is an island entire of itself', and so teamwork in the future will continue to be integral to the effectiveness and success in what we as humans do. That the world is more interconnected through the internet and social media adds further emphasis to this observation and increases the need for us to be aware of and effectively manage the teams that we lead and in which we work.

Bibliography

Adair, J. (1973). *Action-Centred Leadership*. Farnborough, Hants: Gower.

Allan, B. (2019). *The No-Nonsense Guide to Leadership, Management and Teamwork*. London: Facet.

Antonakis, J. (2012). Transformational and charismatic leadership, in D.V. Day and J. Antonakis (Eds), *The Nature of Leadership*. Thousand Oaks, CA: SAGE.

Argyris, C. and Schon, D.A. (1974). *Theory in Practice: Increasing Professional Effectiveness*. San Francisco, CA: Jossey-Bass.

Bales, R.F. (1950). *Interaction Process Analysis: A Method for the Study of Small Groups*. Boston, MA: Addison-Wesley.

Ball, S.J. (2003). The teacher's soul and the terror of performativity, *Journal of Education Policy*, 18:2, 215–228.

Bantel, K.A. and Jackson, S.E. (1989). Top management and innovations in banking: Does the composition of the top team make a difference?, *Strategic Management Journal*, 10:S1, 107–124.

Barnett, K. and McCormick, J. (2012). Leadership and team dynamics in senior executive leadership teams, *Educational Management Administration & Leadership*, 40:6, 653–671.

Barnett, K. and McCormick, J. (2016). Perceptions of task interdependence and functional leadership in schools: Small group research, *The International Journal of Theory, Investigation and Application*, 47:3, 279–302.

Belbin, M. (2010). *Management Teams: Why They Succeed or Fail (3rd edition)*. London: Routledge.

Benoliel, P. (2017). Managing senior management team boundaries and school improvement: An investigation of the school leader role, *International Journal of Leadership in Education*, 20:1, 57–86.

Boyatzis, R.E. (2007). Developing emotional intelligence, in R. Bar-On, K. Maree, J.G. Maree, and M.J. Elias (Eds), *Educating People to Be Emotionally Intelligent*. Westport, CT: Praeger.

Buble, M., Juras, A., and Matic, I. (2014). The relationship between managers' leadership styles and motivation, *Management*, 19:1, 161–193.

Burke, C.S., Stagl, K.C., Klein, C., Goodwin, G.F., Salas, E., and Halpin, S.M. (2006). What type of leadership behaviours are functional in teams? A meta-analysis, *The Leadership Quarterly*, 17:3, 288–307.

Bush, T. (2008). *Leadership and Management Development in Education*. London: Sage.

Bush, T., Abbott, I., Glover, D., Goodall, J., and Smith, R. (2012). *Establishing and Developing High Performing Leadership Teams*. Nottingham: NCSL.

Bush, T. and Glover, D. (2003). *School Leadership: Concepts and Evidence*. Nottingham: NCSL.

Cannon, J. (2016). *Schooling in England 1660–1850: Part 1 'A Noiseless Revolution'*. Croydon: Estate of John Ashton Cannon.

Castka, P., Bamber, C.J., and Sharp, J.M. (2003). Measuring teamwork culture: The use of a modified EFQM model, *Journal of Management Development*, 22:2, 149–170.

Clarke, S. and O'Donoghue, T. (2017). Educational leadership and context: A rendering of an inseparable relationship, *British Journal of Education Studies*, 65:2, 167–182.

Covey, S.R. (2020). *The Seven Habits of Highly Effective People* (30th Anniversary Edition). London: Simon & Schuster.

Cranston, N. and Ehrich, L. (2005). Enhancing the effectiveness of senior management teams in schools, *International Studies in Educational Administration*, 33:1, 79–91.

Cranston, N. and Ehrich, L. (2009). Senior management teams in schools: Understanding their dynamics, enhancing their effectiveness, *Leading and Managing*, 15:1, 14–25.

Crowther, F.S., Ferguson, M., and Hann, L. (2009). *Developing Teacher Leaders: How Teacher Leadership Enhances School Success (2nd edition)*. Thousand Oaks, CA: Corwin.

Currall, L.A., Forrester, R.H. Dawson, J.F. and West, M.A. (2001). It's what you do and the way that you do it: Team task, team size, and innovation-related group processes, *European Journal of Work & Organizational Psychology*, 10:2, 187–204.

Daniels, E., Hondeghem, A., and Dochy, F. (2019). A review on leadership and leadership development in educational settings, *Educational Research Review*, 27, 110–125.

Department for Education (2011). *Teachers' Standards Guidance for School Leaders, School Staff and Governing Bodies*. London: DfE.

Department for Education (2011a). *Education Act, 2011*. London: House of Commons.

Department for Education (2014). *The National Curriculum in England*. London: DfE.

Department for Education (2018). *School Leadership in England 2010 to 2016: Characteristics and Trends*. London: DfE.

Department for Education (2019a). *National Professional Qualification (NPQ) Content and Assessment Framework: A Guide for NPQ Participants*. London: DfE.

Department for Education (2019b). *Achievement of 15-Year-Olds in England: PISA 2018 Results*. London: DfE.

Department for Education (2019c). *Secondary Accountability Measures Guide for Maintained Secondary Schools, Academies, and Free Schools*. London: DfE.

Department for Education (2019d). *Analysis of OfSTED Good and Outstanding Schools*. London: DfE.

Department for Education (2019e). *Teacher Workload Survey 2019*. DfE.

Department for Education (2019f). *School Teachers' Pay and Conditions Document 2019 and Guidance on Schoolteachers' Pay and Conditions*. London: DfE.

Department for Education (2019g). *Teaching Schools and System Leadership: June 2019*. London: DfE.

Department for Education (2020). *National Standards of Excellence for Headteachers*. London: DfE. www.gov.uk/government/publications/national-standards-of-excellence-for-headteachers/headteachers-standards-2020

Department for Education (2021a). *Find and Check the Performance of Schools and Colleges in England*. www.compare-school-performance.service.gov.uk

Department for Education (2021b). *National Professional Qualifications*. London: DfE. www.gov.uk/government/publications/national-professional-qualifications-npqs-refo rms/national-professional-qualifications-npqs-reforms

Department for Education (2021c). *Schools: Statutory Guidance*. London: DfE.

Dering, A., Cunningham, S., and Whitby, K. (2006) Developing leadership teams within an EAZ network: what makes for success? *School Leadership and Management*, 26:2, 107–123.

DeRue, D., Nahrgang, J., Wellman, N., and Humphrey, S. (2011). Trait and behavioural theories of leadership: An integration and meta-analytic test of their relative validity, *Personnel Psychology*, 64, 7–52.

Descartes, R. (1637). *Discourse on the Method*. London: Penguin.

Dimmock, C. and Walker, A. (2000). Cross cultural values and leadership, *Management in Education*, 14:3, 21–24.

Dionne, S.D., Atwater, L.E., and Spangler, W.D. (2004). Transformational leadership and team performance, *Journal of Organisational Change Management*, 17:2, 177–193.

Drach-Zahavy, A. and Somech, A. (2001). Understanding team innovation: The Role of team processes and structures, *Group Dynamics: Theory, Research and Practice*, 5:2, 111–123.

Druskat, V.U. and Pescosolido, A.T. (2002). The content of effective teamwork mental models in self-managing teams: Ownership, learning and heedful interrelating, *in Human Relations*, 55:3, 283–314.

Dube, L. and Robey, D. (2009). Surviving the paradoxes of virtual teamwork, *Information Systems Journal*, 19, 3–30.

Dunham, J. (1995). *Developing Effective School Management*. London: Routledge.

Dunford, J. (2016). *The School Leadership Journey*. Woodbridge: John Catt.

Durant, W. (2006). *The Story of Philosophy: The Lives and Opinions of the Great Philosophers*. New York, NY: Pocket Books.

Dweck, C.S. (2008). *Mindset*. New York, NY: Ballantine Books.

Edmondson, A.C., Roberto, M.A., and Watkins, M.D. (2003). A dynamic model of top management team effectiveness: Managing unstructured task streams, *The Leadership Quarterly*, 14:3, 297–325.

Ehrich, L.C. and Cranston, N. (2004). Developing senior management teams in schools: Can micropolitics help? *International Studies in Educational Administration*, 32:1, 21–31.

Eisenberg, J., Post, C., and DiTomaso, N. (2019). Team dispersion and performance: The role of team communication and transformational leadership, *Small Group Research*, 50:3, 348–380.

Eysenck, H.J. (1966). *Check Your Own I.Q.* London: Penguin.

Fiedler, F.F. (1967). *A Theory of Leadership Effectiveness*. New York, NY, McGraw-Hill.

Gillard, D. (2018). *Education in England: A history*. www.educationengland.org.uk/history/timeline.html

Goleman, D., Boyatzis, R. and McKee, A. (2002). *The New Leaders: Transforming the Art of Leadership into the Science of Results*. London: Little Brown.

Green, H., Facer, K. and Rudd, T. (2005). *Personalisation and Digital Technologies*. London: Nesta.

Grint, K. (2005). *Leadership: Limits and Possibilities*. Basingstoke: Palgrave Macmillan.

Gronn, P. (2002). Distributed leadership, in K. Leithwood and P. Hallinger (Eds), *Second International Handbook of Educational Leadership and Administration*. Dordrecht, The Netherlands: Kulwer.

Gronn, P. (2009). Hybrid Leadership, *in* K. Leithwood, B. Mascall, and T. Strauss (Eds), *Distributed Leadership According to the Evidence*. New York, NY: Routledge.

Hackman, J.R. (2002). From causes to conditions in group research, *Journal of Organisational Behaviour*, 33:3, 428–444.

Hackman, J.R. (2012). *Leading Teams: Setting the Stage for Great Performances*. Boston, MA: Harvard Business School.

Hackman, J.R. and Walton, R.E. (1986). Leading groups in organisations, in P.S. Goodman (Ed.), *Designing Effective Work Groups*. San Francisco: Jossey-Bass.

Hall, V. (2002). From teamwork to teamwork in education, in K. Leithwood and P. Hallinger (Eds), *Second International Handbook of Educational Leadership and Administration*. Dordrecht, The Netherlands: Kulwer.

Hall, V. and Wallace, M. (1996). Let the team take the strain: Lessons from research into senior management teams in secondary schools, *School Organisation*, 16:3, 297–308.

Hallinger, P. (2011). Leadership for learning: Lessons from 40 years of empirical research, *Journal of Educational Administration*, 49:2, 125–142.

Handy, C. (2006). *Understanding Organizations (4th edition)*. London: Penguin.

Harangus, D. and Duda, D.C. (2011). The teamwork abilities versus leadership, *Annals of DAAAM for 2011 & Proceedings of the 22nd International DAAAM Symposium*, 22:1, 381–382.

Harpham, M. (2020). *Progress Plain and Simple: What Every Teacher Needs to Know about Improving Pupil Progress*. London: Routledge.

Harpham, M. (2021). *The School Leader's Year*. London: Routledge.

Harris, A. (2013). Distributed leadership: Friend or foe? *Educational Management, Administration and Leadership*, 41:5, 545–554.

Harris, A. and DeFlaminis, J. (2016). Distributed leadership in practice: Evidence, misconceptions, and possibilities, *Management in Education*, 30:4, 141–146.

Hartle, F. and Thomas, K. (2003). *Growing Tomorrow's School Leaders: The Challenge*. Nottingham: NCSL.

Heifetz, R.A., Grashow, A., and Linsky, M. (2009). *The Practice of Adaptive Leadership*. Boston, MA: Harvard Business School.

Heng-Yu, K., Hung W.T., and Chatchada A. (2013). Collaboration factors, teamwork satisfaction, and student attitudes toward online collaborative learning, *Computers in Human Behavior*, 29:3, 922–929.

Hersey, P. and Blanchard, K.H. (1969). Life cycle theory of leadership, *Training and Development Journal*, 23:5, 26–34.

Herzberg, F., Mausner, B., and Snyderman, B. (1959). *The Motivation to Work (2nd ed.)*. New York, NY: John Wiley.

Hoegl, M. and Gemuenden, G.H. (2001). Teamwork quality and the success of innovative projects: A theoretical concept and empirical evidence, *Organization Science*, 12:4, 435–449.

Honey, P. and Mumford, A. (2000). *The Learning Styles Helper's Guide*. Maidenhead, Berks: Peter Honey Publications.

Hoy, W.K. and Miskel, C.G. (2012). *Educational Administration: Theory, Research and Practice.* Maidenhead: McGraw-Hill.

Huber, S.G. (2004). *Preparing School Leaders for the 21st Century.* London: Routledge.

Hutton, D.M. (2016). Caribbean perspectives, in P. Pashiardis, and O. Johansson (Eds), *Successful School Leadership: International Perspectives.* London: Bloomsbury.

Jameson, J. (2007). *Investigating Collaborative Leadership for Communities of Practice in Learning and Skills. CEL Research Report:* Lancaster, UK: Lancaster University.

Jameson, J. (2015). Leadership in e-learning, in M.J. Spector (Ed.), *The SAGE Encyclopaedia of Educational Technology.* London: Sage.

Jerrim, J. and Sims, S. (2019). *The Teaching and Learning International Survey (TALIS) 2018.* London: UCL.

Kelley, R.E. (1988). In praise of followers, *Harvard Business Review,* (November–December), 142–149.

Kenny, D.A. and Zaccaro, S.J. (1983). An estimate of variance due to traits in leadership, *Journal of Applied Psychology*, 68:4, 678–685.

Kerns, C. (2019). Managing teamwork: A key leadership practice, *Journal of Leadership, Accountability and Ethics,* 16:1, 40–53.

Kickul, J. and Neuman, G. (2000). Emergent leadership behaviours: The function of personality and cognitive ability in determining teamwork performance, *Journal of Business and Psychology,* 15:1, 27–51.

Kingston, P.W., Hubbard, R., Lapp, B., Schroeder, P., and Wilson, J. (2003). Why education matters, *Sociology of Education*, 76:1, 53–70.

Klimoski, R. and Mohammed, S. (1994). Team mental model: Construct or metaphor?, *Journal of Management*, 20:2, 403–437.

Kogler-Hill, S.E. (2016). Team leadership, in P. Northouse (Ed.), *Leadership: Theory and Practice (7th edition).* London: SAGE.

Kolb, D.A. (1984). *Experiential Learning: Experience as the Source of Learning and Development.* Upper Saddle River, NJ: Prentice Hall.

Kouzes, J.M. and Pozner, B.Z. (2017). *The Leadership Challenge: How to Make Extraordinary Things Happen in Organisations (6th edition).* San Francisco, CA: Jossey-Bass.

Kozlowski, S., Watola, D., Jensen, J., Kim, B., and Botero, I. (2009). Developing adaptive teams: A theory of dynamic team leadership, in E. Salas., G. Goodwin, and C. Shawn Burke (Eds.), *Team Effectiveness in Complex Organisations: Cross Disciplinary Perspectives and Approaches.* New York, NY: Psychology Press.

Kur, E. (1996). The faces model of high performing team development, *Leadership and Organisation Development Journal*, 17:1, 32–41.

Larson, C. and LaFasto, F. (1989). *Teamwork: What Must Go Right, What Can Go Wrong.* London: Sage.

Lawler, E.E. (1973). *Motivation in Work Organisations.* Pacific Grove, CA: Brooks Cole.

Leithwood, K., Aitken, R., and Janzi, D. (2006). *Making Schools Smarter: Leading With Evidence.* Thousand Oaks, CA: Corwin.

Levitt, S.R. (2014). Cultural dialectics in international teamwork dynamics, *International Journal of Business Communication,* 56:3, 326–348.

Lord, R., Foti, R. and Phillips, J. (1982). A theory of leadership categorization, in J.G. Hunt, U. Sekaran, and C. Schriesheim (Eds), *Leadership: Beyond Establishment Views.* Carbondale, IL: Southern Illinois University Press.

Lowe, K.B. and Gardner, W.L. (2001). Ten years of the Leadership Quarterly: Contributions and challenges for the future. *Leadership Quarterly*, 11:4, 459–514.

Luthans, F. (2011). *Organisational Behaviour: An Evidence-Based Approach.* Maidenhead: McGraw-Hill.

MacBeath, J., Gray, J., Cullen, J., Frost, D., Steward, S., and Swaffield, S. (2007). *Schools on the Edge: Responding to Challenging Circumstances.* London: Paul Chapman.

MacCrimmon, K.R. (1968). Descriptive and normative implications of the decision-theory postulates, in K. Borch and J. Mossin (Eds), *Risk and Uncertainty. International Economic Association Conference Volumes, Numbers 1–50.* London: Palgrave Macmillan.

Maier, N.R. (1971). Innovation in education, *American Psychologist*, 26:8, 722–725.

Marks, M.A., Mathieu, J.E., DeChurch, L.A., Panzer, F.A., and Alonso, A. (2005). Teamwork in multiteam systems, *Journal of Applied Psychology*, 90:5, 964–971.

Martorell, F., Heaton, P., Gates, S.M., and Hamilton, L.S. (2010). *Preliminary Findings from the New Leaders for New Schools Evaluation.* Santa Monica, CA: RAND.

Maslow, A.H. (1943). A theory of human motivation, *Psychological Review*, 50(4), 370–396.

Mathieu, J.E., Heffner, T.S., Goodwin, G.F., Salas, E., and Cannon-Bowers, J.A. (2000). The influence of shared mental models on team process and performance, *Journal of Applied Psychology*, 85:2, 273–283.

McIntyre, H.H. and Foti, R.J. (2013). The impact of shared leadership on teamwork mental models and performance in self-directed teams, *Group Processes & Intergroup Relations*, 16:1, 46–57.

Mehra, A., Smith, B., Dixon, A., and Robertson, B. (2006). Distributed leadership in teams: The network of leadership perceptions and team performance, *Leadership Quarterly*, 17, 232–245.

Meindl, J.R. (1995). The romance of leadership as a follower-centric theory: A social constructionist approach, *The Leadership Quarterly*, 6:3, 329–341.

Mestry, R. (2016). African perspectives, in P. Pashiardis, and O. Johansson (Eds), *Successful School Leadership: International Perspectives.* London: Bloomsbury.

Miller, P.M. (2016). Developing successful and effective school leadership: Caribbean perspectives, in P. Pashiardis, and O. Johansson (Eds), *Successful School Leadership: International Perspectives.* London: Bloomsbury.

Mitchell, C. and Sackney, L. (2000). *Profound Improvement: Building Capacity for a Learning Community.* Abingdon: Swets & Zeitlinger.

Mitgang, L. (2012). *The Making of the Principal: Five Lessons in Leadership Training.* New York, NY: Wallace Foundation.

Morgeson, F., DeRue, D., and Karam, E. (2010). Leadership in teams: A functional approach to understanding leadership structures and processes. *Journal of Management*, 36, 5–39.

Morrison, K. (2002). *School Leadership and Complexity Theory.* London: Routledge.

Moswela, B. and Kgosidialwa, K. (2019). Leadership and school success: Barriers to leadership in Botswana primary and secondary schools, *Educational Management Administration & Leadership*, 47:3, 443–456.

Murphy, J. (2005). *Connecting Teacher Leadership and School Improvement.* Thousand Oaks, CA: Corwin.

Myers, I. (1978). *Myers-Briggs Type Indicator.* Palo Alto, CA: Consulting Psychologists Press.

Myerson, R.B. (1991). Basic concepts of decision theory, in *Game Theory Analysis of Conflict.* Cambridge, MA: Harvard University Press.

Neumann, A. (1991). The thinking team: Toward a cognitive model of administrative teamwork in higher education, *Journal of Higher Education*, 623:5, 485–513.

Northouse, P. (2016). *Leadership: Theory and Practice (7th edition)*. London: SAGE.

O'Donoghue, T. and Clarke, S. (2010). *Leading Learning: Process, Themes, and Issues in International Contexts*. London: Routledge.

Ofsted (2019a). *School Inspection Handbook*. London: Ofsted.

Ofsted (2019b). *Multi-academy Trusts: Benefits, Challenges, and Functions*. London: Ofsted.

Ofsted (2019c). *Teacher Wellbeing at Work in Schools and Further Education Providers*. London: Ofsted.

Ofsted (2020). *The Annual Report of Her Majesty's Chief Inspector of Education, Children's Services and Skills 2019/20*. London: Ofsted.

Owens, R.E. and Valesky, T.C. (2006). *Organisational Behaviour in Education: Adaptive Leadership and School Reform (9th edition)*. New York, NY: Pearson.

Oxford English Dictionary, (2009). *The Pocket Oxford English Dictionary*. Oxford: Oxford University Press.

Parker, G.M. (2008). *Team Players and Teamwork*. San Francisco, CA: Wiley.

Pashiardis, P. and Johansson, O. (2016). *Successful School Leadership: International Perspectives*. London: Bloomsbury.

Pastor, J., Meindl, J.R., and Mayo, M.C. (2002), A network effects model of charisma attributions, *Academy of Management Journal*, 45:2, 410–420.

Pont, B., Nusches, D., and Moorman, H. (2008). *Improving School Leadership Volume 1: Policy and Practice*. Paris: OECD.

Qiu, M. and McDougall, D. (2013). Foster strengths and weaknesses: Advantages and disadvantages of online versus face-to-face subgroup discourse, *Computers and Education*, 67, 1–11.

Radcliffe, S. (2012). *Leadership Plain and Simple (2nd edition)*. London: Pearson.

Raja, R. and Nagasubramani, P.C. (2018). Impact of modern technology on education, *Journal of Applied and Advanced Research*, 3:1 S33–S35.

Rasmussen, T.H. and Jeppesen, H.J. (2006). Teamwork and associated psychological factors: A review, *Work & Stress*, 20, 105–128.

Razik, T. and Swanson, A. (2010). *Fundamental Concepts of Educational Leadership and Management*. Boston, MA: Allyn & Bacon.

Riaz, N. and Sultan, S. (2017). What is under the layer: Leadership practices of public school headteachers in Pakistan, *FWU Journal of Social Sciences*, 11:2, 201–213.

Rickards, T. and Moger, S. (2000). Creative leadership processes in project team development: An alternative to Tuckman's stage model, *British Journal of Management*, 11, 273–283.

Robson, C. and McCartan, K. (2016). *Real World Research (4th edition)*. Chichester: Wiley.

Rocco, T.S. and Plakhotnik, M.S. (2009). Literature reviews, conceptual frameworks, and theoretical frameworks: Terms, functions, and distinctions, *Human Resource Development Review*, 8:1, 120–130.

Rogers, G. and Badham, L. (1992). *Evaluation in Schools: Getting Started on Training and Implementation*. London: Routledge.

Salas, E., Rosen, M.A., Burke, C.S., and Goodwin, G.F. (2009). The wisdom of collectives in organizations: An update of the teamwork competencies, in *Team Effectiveness in*

Complex Organizations: Cross-disciplinary Perspectives and Approaches. New York, NY: Routledge.

Sammons, P., Hillman, J., and Mortimore, P. (1995). *Key Characteristics of Effective Schools: A Review of School Effectiveness Research.* London: Institute of Education, University of London.

Scheerens, J. (2012). *School Leadership Effects Revisited: Review and Meta-analysis of Empirical Studies.* London: Springer.

Schleicher, A. (2006). *The Economics of Knowledge: Why Education Is Key for Europe's Success.* Paris: OECD.

Senior, B. and Swailes, S. (2007). Inside management teams: Developing a teamwork survey instrument, *British Journal of Management,* 18, 138–153.

Sennett, R. (1998). *The Corrosion of Character: The Personal Consequences of Work in the New Capitalism.* New York, NY: Norton.

Sergiovanni, T. (2001). *Leadership: What's in It for Schools?* London: Routledge.

Sheard, G., Kakebase, A., and Kakebase, N. (2009). *Leadership Teams: Developing and Sustaining High Performance.* Basingstoke, Hants: Palgrave Macmillan.

Shenoy, V., Mahendra, S., and Vijay, N. (2020). COVID 19 – lockdown: Technology adaption, teaching, learning, students engagement and faculty experience, in *Mukt Shabd Journal,* 9:4, 698–702.

Shuffler, M. (2013). *Where's The Boss? The Influences of Emergent Team Leadership Structures on Team Outcomes in Virtual and Distributed Environments. Electronic Theses and Dissertations,* 2004–2019, University of Central Florida.

Sinclair, A. (1992). The tyranny of a team ideology, *Organisation Studies,* 13:4, 611–626.

Smyth, J. (2006). Educational leadership that fosters 'student voice', *International Journal of Leadership in Education,* 9:4, 279–284.

Solomon, Y. and Lewin, C. (2016). Measuring 'progress': Performativity as both driver and constraint in school innovation, *Journal of Education Policy,* 31:2, 226–238.

Spillane, J.P. (2012). *Distributed Leadership.* San Francisco, CA: Jossey-Bass.

Stello, C.M. (2011). *Herzberg's Two-Factor Theory of Job Satisfaction: An Integrative Literature Review.* Paper presented at the 2011 Student research Conference, University of Minnesota, MN.

Stott, K. and Walker, A. (1995). *Teams, Teamwork & Teambuilding: The Manager's Complete Guide to Teams in Organisations.* New York, NY: Prentice Hall.

Supovitz, J. and Riggan, M. (2012). Building a foundation for school leadership: An evaluation of the Annenberg Distributed Leadership Project, 2006–2010. In *Consortium for Policy Research in Education,* University of Pennsylvania, Philadelphia, PA.

Tannenbaum, R. and Schmidt, W.H. (2008). *How to Choose a Leadership Pattern.* Boston: Harvard Business School.

Tannenbaum, S.I., Traylor, A.M., and Thomas, E.J. (2021). Managing teamwork in the face of pandemic: Evidence-based tips, *BMJ Qual Saf,* 30:1, 59–63.

Thompson, L.F. and Coovert, M.D. (2003). Teamwork online: The effects of computer conferencing on perceived confusion, satisfaction, and post discussion accuracy, *Group Dynamics: Theory, Research, and Practice,* 7:2, 135–151.

Tian, M., Risku, M., and Collin, K. (2016). A meta-analysis of distributed leadership from 2002 to 2013: Theory development, empirical evidence, and future research focus, *Educational Management Administration & Leadership,* 44:1, 146–164.

Timperley, H.S. (2005). Distributed leadership: Developing theory from practice, *Journal of Curriculum Studies*, 37:4, 395–420.

Tuckman, B.W. and Jensen, M.C. (1977). Stages of small-group development revisited, *Group & Organizational Studies,* 2, 419–427.

Van Den Bossche, P., Gijselaers, W.H., Segers, M., and Kirschner, P.A. (2006). Social and cognitive factors driving teamwork in collaborative learning environments team learning beliefs and behaviours, *Small Group Research,* 37:5, 490–521.

Varela, D.G. and Fedynich, L. (2020). Leading schools from a social distance: Surveying South Texas school district leadership during the COVID-19 pandemic, *National Forum of Educational Administration and Supervision Journal*, 38:4, 1–10.

Vroom, V.H. (1964). *Work and Motivation.* New York, NY: Wiley.

Vroom, V.H. and Jago, A.G. (1988). *The New Leadership: Managing Participation in Organizations.* Englewood Cliffs, NJ: Prentice-Hall.

Vroom, V.H. and Yetton, P.W. (1973). *Leadership and Decision Making.* Pittsburgh, PA: University of Pittsburgh Press.

Wageman, R., Nunes, D.A., Burruss, J.A., and Hackman, J.R. (2008). *Senior Leadership Teams: What It Takes to Make Them Great.* Boston, MA: Harvard Business School.

Wallace, M. (2001). Sharing leadership of schools through teamwork a justifiable risk?, *Educational Management & Administration,* 29:2 153–167.

Westerbeek, H. and Smith, A. (2005). *Business Leadership and the Lessons for Sport.* Basingstoke: Palgrave Macmillan.

Wiyono, B.B. (2018). The effect of self-evaluation on the principals' transformational leadership, teachers' work motivation, teamwork effectiveness, and school improvement, *International Journal of Leadership in Education,* 21:6, 705–725.

Wright, D.K. (2005). Researching internet-based populations: Advantages and disadvantages of online survey research, online questionnaire authoring software packages, and web survey services, *Journal of Computer-Mediated Communication*, 10:3, 1083–1091.

Yang, L-R., Huang, C-H., and Wu, K-S. (2010). The association among project manager's leadership style, teamwork, and project success, *International Journal of Project Management,* 29, 258–267.

Yukl, G. (2013). *Leadership in Organisations.* New York, NY: Pearson.

Zaccaro, S.J., Heinen, B., and Shuffler, M. (2008). *Team Leadership and Team Effectiveness.* London: Routledge.

Zaccaro, S.J., Rittman, A.L., and Marks, M.A. (2001). Team leadership, *Leadership Quarterly*, 12, 451–483.

Index

Note: Page numbers in *italics* indicate figures.